W. S. MERWIN THE MYTHMAKER

MARK CHRISTHILF

# W. S. MERWIN THE MYTHMAKER

A LITERARY FRONTIERS EDITION, NO. 26
UNIVERSITY OF MISSOURI PRESS
COLUMBIA, 1986

AAX 9894

PS
3563
E75
Z63
1986

8/19...
am...

Library of Congress Cataloging-in-Publication Data

Christhilf, Mark.
    W. S. Merwin, the mythmaker

    (A Literary frontiers edition)
    Bibliography: p.
    1. Merwin, W. S. (William Stanley), 1927-    —Criti-
cism and interpretation.    2. Myth in literature.
3. Mythology in literature.    I. Title.    II. Series.
PS3563.E75Z63   1986      811'.54      85–20123
ISBN 0-8262-0478-3 (alk. paper)

# CONTENTS

I. Myth and Poetry, 1

II. A Myth of History, 17

III. Reclaiming Mythic Consciousness, 31

IV. The Myth of an Original World, 47

V. A Mythic Image of Humankind, 61

Works by W. S. Merwin, 77

# I. MYTH AND POETRY

The poetry of the American writer W. S. Merwin belongs to both modernist and postmodernist traditions of literature. Written from 1952 to 1960, his first four volumes reveal the influence of such modernist poets as T. S. Eliot, W. B. Yeats, and Robert Graves. With his fifth volume, *The Moving Target* (1963), Merwin transformed his poetic style, contributing to a definition of the emergent postmodernist aesthetics. Yet Merwin's commentators often overlook the way in which his poetry connects the two traditions. Eager to concentrate on the postmodern phase, they break his poetic career into halves, ignoring the relation of early to later poetry. One commentator observes, "There seem to be two poets named Merwin, each very prolific and wonderfully accomplished, but what do they share?"[1]

What the two Merwins share is a vitalizing concern with the relationship of poetry and mythology. In a foreword to Merwin's first volume, *A Mask for Janus* (1952), W. H. Auden noticed that the poems reflect "the eternal relevance to the human condition of the great myths." Nearly twenty years later in a 1970 interview, Merwin responded to a comment that his poetry had lost the "mythological cast" to which Auden called attention. Discouraging the view that his later poems forego contact with mythology, he stated: "Often I try to do something that is not mythological, but it turns out that in some way or other I find I am recreating the conditions of mythology."[2]

The general subject of this study is the way in which Merwin re-creates "conditions of mythology." My thesis is that his poetry eventually assimilates both the purpose and the method of mythic thought. In *A Mask for Janus, The*

1. Daniel Hoffman, "The Gift of Tongues: W. S. Merwin's Poems and Translations," *Hollins Critic* 5 (1968):3.
2. Frank McShane, "A Portrait of W. S. Merwin," *Shenandoah* 21 (1970):12.

1

*Dancing Bears* (1954), and *Green with Beasts* (1956), Merwin discovers that myth and poetry have the same objectives: both direct attention to humankind's unity with the cosmos. To give this purpose relevance as his career developed, Merwin improvised myth's traditionally narrative pattern and appropriated its essential method of explaining events solely by means of imagination. In the poems of *The Moving Target* through those of *The Compass Flower* (1977), the poet assumes the role of mythmaker: he gives imaginative order to the world, to history, and to individual existence. Finally, ambivalence toward this role informs the latest books, *Finding the Islands* (1982) and *Opening the Hand* (1983).

When Merwin began writing, mythology and poetry were closely related. Modernist poets viewed myths as an ancient poetry forming the bedrock of culture. Anonymous stories, orally transmitted, myths revealed the wisdom and self-image of a people. This literary attitude was part of an encompassing, twentieth-century movement to study the human past in order to discover universal patterns of behavior. Mythographers such as Sir James Frazer compared myths of primitive cultures to Classical and Christian mythologies of the West and, by revealing similarities, exposed what they considered the provincialism of Western thought. It is well known that Frazer's findings influenced modernist writers. More generally, emphasis on universal human behavior led poets to identify readily with experience embodied in the cultural past. Repetition, therefore, defines the relationship of the modernist poem to myth: mythic narratives and legends could be successfully improvised because there was little difference between experience portrayed in them and contemporary experience. A widely used modernist form was the dramatic monologue in which the poet assumes a mythic identity analogous to his contemporary situation. Through this act of identification he achieves liberation from personal existence.

The modernist viewpoint would have been stimulating to a young poet emerging from college in 1948, especially to one who desired to rectify his own provincialism. With

2

roots in the American-German middle class of rural western Pennsylvania, Merwin felt self-conscious about his lack of cultural experience. Much later in his career he was to suggest the authority that culture represented to him: "Coming from my own provincial and utterly unliterary background, I was overly impressed with Culture (with a capital C)."[3] Abetting Merwin's feeling of provincialism was the tradition of Christian Presbyterianism in which he was raised by his father—a minister. Merwin has characterized his father's family as culturally impoverished and intimated that his father himself personified an oppressively narrow and dogmatic religious tradition. What glimpses he did have of culture came through his mother (*Unframed Originals*, 177). In fact, Merwin's decision to become a poet may have derived from his desire to supplant the authority of his paternal religion with a more supreme authority. That he came to regard cultural tradition as a means of liberation from the inhibiting effect of the Christian mythological system is implied in his description of his earliest attempts to write under his father's strict tutelage: "I started writing hymns for my father almost as soon as I could write at all. . . . rather stern little pieces addressed, in a manner I was familiar with, to backsliders, but I can remember too wondering whether there might not be some liberating mode."[4]

Merwin left America soon after college to pursue the "liberating mode." Following the example of Henry James and T. S. Eliot, he became an expatriate, living in England until 1957 and in France during the 1960s. Following the advice of Ezra Pound, Merwin immersed himself in the study of foreign languages and cultures in order to universalize his poetic idiom. Determination to liberate himself from provincialism through assimilation of mankind's cultural history resounds in such early poems from *A Mask for*

3. Ed Folsom and Cary Nelson, "'Fact Has Two Faces': An Interview with W. S. Merwin," *Iowa Review* 13 (1982):30.

4. James M. Ethridge and Barbara Kopola, eds., *Contemporary Authors: A Bio-Bibliographic Guide to Current Authors and Their Works* (Detroit: Gale, 1966), 299.

*Janus* as "Anabasis I," "Anabasis II," and "Ballad of John Cable and Three Gentlemen." The latter poem tells a story about a provincial man, John Cable, who lives in a community with his wife, mother, and sister. He is summoned one day by three gentlemen who appear in a boat on "a gray river / Wide as the sea" and demand that Cable come away with them. Speaking as one person, the gentlemen represent the Muse, for they want Cable to accompany them to a place that is clearly a Byzantium—a city of art in which mankind's spiritual life subsumes the individual's existence.

Initially Cable resists leaving his materialistic domestic life. He offers excuses to the gentlemen, but they refute each of them, finally persuading him to depart for the city of art. As Cable appears a type for the poet and his conflict, Merwin's ballad discloses the Romantic conception of aesthetic vocation informing the modernist view. The artist must be different from others, committing himself to the family of humankind, rather than to a personal family. The task of making experience intelligible—the mythopoeic task—necessitates impersonality and exile. To use the words of James Joyce, the Irish modernist whom Merwin admired, the artist will become a "priest of imagination," transmuting daily experience. This note of austere loneliness and difficult grandeur can be heard in the final image of "John Cable" as aesthetic vocation is accepted:

> Now Cable is carried
> On the dark river;
> Nor even a shadow
> Followed him over.
>
> On the wide river
> Gray as the sea
> Flags of white water
> Are his company. (18)

Merwin's feeling for the authority of the cultural past was deepened by his association with Robert Graves at the beginning of his career. In Majorca in 1950 while tutoring

Graves's children, Merwin made direct contact with one of the most Romantic viewpoints in the modernist tradition. In the current of modernism represented by Graves—and by Yeats and Edwin Muir—there is total repudiation of contemporary history and equally total affirmation of the mythological habit of mind. For these writers modern history since the Enlightenment was a false direction because of the stress on reasoning consciousness and on the acceptance of scientific materialism. Intellectual progress discredited an imaginative response to the world—the source both of myth and of poetry. These poets found inspiration in the Celto-Germanic mythology that was the predominant European belief until the Roman era and that survived in the folk tales of Ireland and Wales.[5]

Graves had just perfected his prose version of this mythology when Merwin associated with him. A work with a comparative approach not unlike Frazer's, Graves's *The White Goddess: A Historical Grammar for Poetry* (1966) asserts the importance of the ancient belief in a female deity—a moon goddess who controls the natural processes of seasonal change, birth and death, creation and destruction. It describes the rites of primitive matrilineal cultures in which kings, who embodied the waxing and waning spirit of the year, were sacrificed twice yearly to gain the favor of the goddess. In the central mythic tale the soul of the sacrificed "sun-king" would inhabit a royal purgatory—an island or garden beyond the sea, where it would await renewal in the waxing half of the year. Graves reasoned that the poet should identify with the captive sun-king: he should make the goddess his muse and prove his love for her by invoking her presence in what was clearly a waning period of history. In turn she might bring about a "waxing year"—a period of renewal when mankind would reaffirm the primacy of imagination.

The White Goddess mythology appealed to Merwin's

5. Daniel Hoffman, *Barbarous Knowledge: Myth in the Poetry of Yeats, Graves, Muir* (New York: Oxford University Press, 1967), 19–20.

idealism and to his predisposition for cultural authority. More than any other mythological tradition, the ancient story of the goddess and her kings dominates the poetry of *A Mask for Janus* and *The Dancing Bears*. This is not apparent immediately, for Merwin's ostensible tendency is to take inspiration from all mythological traditions and to synthesize their details. Mythic heroes and legends are represented from Classical, Hebraic, and Christian traditions: in dramatic monologues the poet revivifies such figures as the Greek hero Perseus in "Ode: The Medusa Face," the biblical Jacob in "Colloquy at Peniel," or the Christian Magi in "Carol of the Three Kings." To be sure, Merwin's attitude toward myth is generally one of exploration; as Alice Benston notices, until *The Drunk in the Furnace* (1960) Merwin's habit is "to explore the common ground of all myths and not to give weight to the particular truth of a single tradition."[6] Yet in his first two volumes there is abundant evidence that the story of the goddess preoccupied Merwin: when retelling the mythic tales of other cultures, he substitutes pantheistic Celto-Germanic imagery. Also, there is allusion to the story—as story—in several poems. In "Variation on a Line by Emerson," in *A Mask for Janus*, Merwin identifies explicitly with the legend of the sleeping sun-king:

> Let a kind diction out of the shadows tell,
> Now toward my slumber, a legend unto my face
> Of sleep as a quiet garden without malice
>
> . . . . . . . . . . . . . . . . . . . . . . . . . .
> So let me lie in a story, heavy with evening. (30)

Merwin conceives diverse poetic strategies for retelling this mythic tale. In a few poems he simply describes the goddess as an object of love: she is a lady or maiden whose attributes include prophetic birds, especially herons; the number three, for she has three appearances; and a wheel

6. "Myth in the Poetry of W. S. Merwin," in *Poets in Progress: Critical Prefaces to Thirteen Modern American Poets*, ed. Edward Hungerford (Evanston: Northwestern University Press, 1967), 195.

that she turns to reconcile creation and destruction. Merwin gives her a voice in a number of early poems, indicating sympathy with Graves's view that she exists in humanity's unconscious memory. Because in sleep such memories reassert their influence, in "Song with the Eyes Closed" the muse-goddess proclaims: "I am the shape of sleep." In other songlike poems the shrill quality of her voice reveals Merwin's interest in her identity as the nightmare; in "Margery's Song" she is clearly Cardea, the mistress of Janus, a Roman agricultural king. According to one legend, Cardea, whose sacred tree was the hawthorn, changed herself into a bird and tried to eat her children. Thus she sings:

> I am a jill-whisper
> And a cold sister
> And a windy daughter
> With hawthorn in my hair.
> . . . . . . . . . . . . . . . . .
> A nimble bird I saw:
> Ruses were its children;
> And friendly was the wind
> But spoke me hungerly. (80)

Although there are exceptions, Merwin's general interest is in the goddess as Cardea—as a queen of the woods and moon—in *A Mask for Janus*; in *The Dancing Bears* he portrays her as a Celtic Aphrodite, queen of the sea.

Both early volumes include poems in which Merwin addresses his muse-goddess. She is the "Lady" addressed in the "Song" at the end of *A Mask for Janus* and in "Canso" at the end of *The Dancing Bears*. In these poems Merwin assumes "a mask" for Janus the sun-king, and in "Festival" he is explicit about this identification, declaring "I that am king of no country." Specifically Merwin retells the mythic episode in which the sun-king lies in purgatory, entombed in the garden or castle of the goddess. In order to avoid direct ideological statement, Merwin takes this mythical condition to express the poet's historical situation. Like the sun-king, the poet is dispossessed and must passively endure, awaiting renewal. The reasons for the poet's purgatorial condition are heard clearly in "Cancion y Glosa," a poem with an epigraph by Juan Ramón Jiménez, the Spanish Nobel Prize–winning poet whom Merwin was translating. Addressing a lady with whom he seeks to identify, the speaker tabulates the "disstated things" in the "vain country" from which he would avert his gaze. In contemporary history, Merwin intimates, there is no belief in imagination and, therefore, no reverence and no wonder:

> There is no breath of days
> in that time where I was,
> in that place, through the trees;
> . . . . . . . . . . . . . . . . . . .
> nor any dance to please,
> nor prayers, pleasure of knees,
> . . . . . . . . . . . . . . . . . .
> and no shadow-plays,
> trepidation of fingers,
> ruse of limbs or faces,
> ghosts nor histories. (47–48)

The mythic theme of a purgatory accounts for much of the imagery in *A Mask for Janus*, and for the mood of languor that consequently pervades the book. For instance, Merwin employs a motif of sleep, suggesting repose and waiting. In "Herons" a narrator begins the poem's events by stating, "I slept, and the hour and shadow slept." Merwin also conveys the purgatorial condition through motifs of blindness, darkness, and shadow—all of which express the sun-king-poet's lack of power in a "waning" or dark period of history. Since there is "no light" or idealism, the three kings in "Carol of the Three Kings" declare, "We have been blindness / Between sun and moon." Imagery of shadows is most prevalent and more complicated than that of darkness and blindness. The shadow expresses the bodiless and enervated condition of the sun-king; but it is also used more generally as a mythic symbol to represent imagination and spirit—the nonmaterialistic side of life. In this sense the shadow is to be embraced: through belief in shadows there will be renewal. "Blind William's Song" is a poem with evident autobiographical reference since William is Merwin's first name; in it the blind speaker swears indifference to the sights of the "middle earth"—his own historical period. Identifying his shadow with a "white dream" who is evidently his muse, he asserts: "Stand from my shadow where it goes / Threaded upon a white dream."

"East of the Sun and West of the Moon," a poem of over five hundred lines in *The Dancing Bears* is Merwin's most sustained illustration of the White Goddess myth. Although it can be read as a version of the Cupid and Psyche story or as a tale of a lost and regained Christian paradise, the key to its images and details is Celtic folklore. Omnisciently narrated, the poem begins in winter with a white bear—"a white and monstrous thing"—who woos a peasant girl. When she agrees to marry him, he takes her to his palace and tells her that for a year he must remain disguised because of "the ministrations of an evil stepdame." Actually, he is a sun-king, this stepdame is the muse-goddess, and he and the girl must undergo a period of waiting with patience. Although he begs for her trust and identification, the girl fails him, stealing at night to see him as he is truly, a "prince shaming with beauty / The sun peerless at noon." As a result of her betrayal the bear-prince is taken to the "wheeling castle" of his mother, which lies on an island beyond the sea—"east of the sun and west of the moon." Realizing her loss, the girl is able through repeated labors to make her way to the island and to awaken the prince who sleeps there in his purgatory. As the poem ends with their reunion, it is evident that the girl represents the poet who successfully identifies with the sun-king. Together they stand for a period of renewal; in the words of the bear-prince, "we are the sense of dawn beneath pretence / Of an order of darkness."

Much of the interest of "East of the Sun" lies in Merwin's use of the girl as poet. Through her Merwin indicates that love is imagination: love enables the poet to believe the story of an all-powerful muse. Before she betrays love by failing to imagine, the girl in the bear's palace is clearly

in the palace of art. A place without motion or sound—
"where no shrub grew, / Nor grass rustled"—it is elegant
but artificial. As she yearns for the mutable world, the girl
expresses Merwin's fatigue with art centered exclusively on
the cultural past. By lamenting that she must live "in some
ancestral fantasy," she suggests that he is dissatisfied with
simply retelling the muse's story—and with the mask of the
sun-king informing his early poetic voice.

\*    \*    \*

In the poetry of *Green with Beasts* and *The Drunk in the
Furnace*, the world becomes a predominant subject. Eliminating arcane references to island gardens and wheeling
castles, Merwin concentrates on the actual topography of
the creation—on its mountains, rivers, and seas. This
emerging sense of identity with Creation, and the means of
its articulation, were to provide him with a challenge for
the remainder of his career. Feeling for the world would
have followed naturally from his predilection for pantheistic mythology. Further, to an extent all mythologies
have one essential feature, one common story: all depict
the penetration of the natural and visible world by a hidden
power, and this creative event gives order and reality to the
world and to the life on it. As the authority of culture
abates in Merwin's perspective, it is this mythological conception of the world that increasingly informs his poetry.

A mythic world view is implied in Merwin's essay on the
poetry of Dylan Thomas, entitled "The Religious Poet." Revealing admiration for Thomas, whom he calls "a major
poet of our century," Merwin also develops the notion of
the religious artist as a type. Thomas's poetry is founded
on a religious vision and on a corollary power to make
myth, Merwin argues, because he was able to perceive
"Creation as divine" and to understand "love as God" (64).
In Merwin's perspective the role of love is critical, and it
suggests his affinity not simply with Thomas but with such
poets as Jiménez and especially with the Platonic mythology preserved in medieval thought. In this tradition love is

10

the divine creative force from which the world was called into being. It is a spiritual principle energizing nature that Merwin imagines in his poem "The Saphire" as "the world's love before the world was." As a creative force, love also renews the world, making it appear beautiful; in human experience it compels feeling for the world and the desire to merge with absolute beauty. Intuition of this spiritual force, Merwin claims, will persuade the artist to become "a celebrator":

> That which he celebrates is Creation. . . . In both man and the world he will perceive a force of love or creation which is more divine than either man or the world, and a force of death or destruction which is more terrible than man or the world. . . . in the act of love, the central act of Creation, he will see the force of love, in man and the world, merge inextricably and mysteriously with the force of death, and yet from this union new creation. (59–60)

To celebrate, then, means to tell the story of love's influence in the world—the story of "A world's unknown dimension," as Merwin expresses it in an early poem. Often he symbolizes the story of love as a song: it is the music of cosmic unity, arising from the harmony of all created things. Merwin's desire to become a vessel for this song is revealed implicitly in such poems of *Green with Beasts* as "Saint Sebastian" and "The Annunciation"—poems in which he identifies with mythic characters who have experienced the love. In "The Annunciation," Christ's mother Mary has felt "love as God" and seeks words for what is ultimately an ineffable experience:

> . . . the way the silence
> Was hearing, like it was hearing a great song
> And the song was hearing the silence forever
> And forever and ever . . . (150)

Merwin's effort to direct the reader's attention to Creation's eternal song is an attempt to inculcate wonder, and it culminates in *Green with Beasts* before declining in *The Drunk in the Furnace*. By taking as his subject the origin of Creation and mankind's relation to it, he appropriates into his poetry the function of mythology. For according to the mythographer Joseph Campbell, in all myth the individual is identified with a transcendent and meaningful cosmos embodying a creative principle: "The individual is thereby united with the way of nature . . . in accord with the wonder of the whole."[7]

Appearing frequently in Merwin's account of an eternal Creation are the symbols and the imagery of the world's oldest mythological system. Informing both Celto-Germanic and Platonic mythologies, primitive Asian myth portrays a cosmos given meaning by an original unity between heaven and earth. As a result of the Fall, heaven and earth fell apart, but remained connected at the earth's center—the still point of the turning world. From this point, a void or primordial chaos, creation of the world continued and all things returned to it. In his poems Merwin imagines this experience as one in which the world seems to stand still before turning forward again. As the source of renewal, the still point is figured as poetic inspiration in Merwin's dedication to *Green with Beasts*, where he claims that his poems arise unbidden from a "still place of perpetual surprise." Merwin sometimes uses imagery literally suggestive of the void to communicate experience of this place: it is a violent sensation of fire and light, darkness and thunder, and beating of wings. Emptiness and distance, silence and stillness are more often the images that evoke, through negation, the world's invisible dimension.

Under the inspiration of Asian mythology Merwin asserts the world's significance in "The Mountain," in *Green with Beasts*. He describes a huge mountain apparently different from other peaks by virtue of its height and "its centrality." Portraying the slopes that are lost in the clouds,

7. "Myths from East to West," in *Myths*, by Alexander Eliot, with contributions by Mircea Eliade and Joseph Campbell (New York: McGraw-Hill, 1976), 35.

Merwin claims that "only on the rarest occasions" can one see above the treeline. And were there no clouds, Merwin continues, it would still be impossible to see the mountain's summit, for such vast natural shapes transcend the human being's perceptual capacity—"for at the distance at which in theory / One could see it all, it would be out of sight." As he relates the failed attempts to scale the mountain and gain the summit, it is evident that he has in mind the Asian legend that one tall mountain united earth to heaven at its summit, the center of the world. Thus Merwin describes conditions on the upper slopes in images suggesting the still point: "the whole aspect and condition / Of the mountain changes completely; there is ceaseless wind / With a noise like thunder and the beating of wings." Relating accounts of the climbers who went farthest, Merwin notices the "characteristic / Effects of the upper slopes" as an experience of eternity: "of time / Passed there not passing here, which we could not understand, / Of time no time at all."

Because "The Mountain" is structured around an investigation of the legends inspired by it, the poem suggests the development of Merwin's attitude toward myths. In one stanza Merwin recounts the legend that "it will fall on us" and the countervening belief that "It has already fallen." He reacts with indifference to the actual veracity of either legend; through a question he implies that what is important is to see in the mountain the world's eternal dimension. "Have we not / Seen it fall in shadow," he queries, "evening after evening, / Across everything we can touch." It is this act of imaginative identification with the world that calls forth wonder. Thus Merwin continues by affirming the various tales that the mountain evokes: "even the old woman / Who laughs, pointing, and says that the clouds across / Its face are wings of seraphim." In all such imaginative responses to the Creation, human beings conceive their origins and their continuing unity with Creation. Stressing this unity, Merwin describes the bafflingly vertical experience of the mountain slope as very much like mankind's experience of himself. Because mankind is a natural creature who experiences "higher" ontological being, Merwin states:

> ... it seems probable
> Sometimes that the slope, to be so elusive
> And yet so inescapable, must be nothing
> But ourselves ... (154)

*Green with Beasts* concludes with a section of eight poems whose subject is the sea, and it is followed by *The Drunk in the Furnace*, whose first twelve pieces are also sea poems. Numbering twenty in all, these stories and sagas describe expeditions and shipwrecks in a dramatic mode in which the speaker, for the most part, is a mariner among a ship's crew. Set in a premodern era, they were probably inspired by Merwin's play "Favor Island" (1957), which narrates a voyage in the eighteenth century from England to Ireland. The sea in the poems is both a setting and a mythic metaphor: an image for Merwin's belief in the myth of Creation's ideal forces. In the sea poems of *Green with Beasts* he clearly intends to celebrate in the sea the mysterious presence of love and death. For instance, in "Shipwreck" an awful storm brings death to the mariners, but their deaths appear meaningful since they are part of an eternal order. In "Leviathan" the sea obviously embodies the Creation's principle of love and renewal:

> ... The sea curling,
> Star-climbed, wind-combed, cumbered with itself still
> As at first it was, is the hand not yet contented
> Of the Creator ... (128)

Merwin weaves into his sea poems a mythic theme of exploration and gives the theme a dual reference. He uses mankind's attempt to chart the seas as an index of human idealism and capability in the manner in which it has been traditionally portrayed in myth and literature. Sea exploration is also an analogue for Merwin's poetic purpose: it signifies a personal effort to find inspiration in nature. For the poet-explorer the sea should contain "A world's unknown dimension"—the possibility that the world's depth and distance will replenish creative perception. This double theme is evident in Merwin's "Fog," in which the mariners, in order to be safe, have been "shore-hugging." Dreaming of life on land, they have not been alert and have been suddenly enveloped by blinding fog. After considering their confusion and lack of direction, the speaker-helmsman berates himself and his fellows for their lack of spirit. He states that to be saved from the fog all that one needs to know is "which way deep water lies." Echoing Merwin's feeling that the natural world is inspiriting, the mariner advises the crew: "Let us turn head, / Out oars, and pull for the open. Make we / For mid-sea, where the winds are and stars too."

Gradually, however, the sea lost its power of inspiration for Merwin, an event that signaled his diminishing capacity as celebrator. Merwin began to suspect that the historical process is not influenced by Creation's forces and that mankind's unity with the world is not guaranteed. Disillusionment is evident in the sea poems of *The Drunk in the Furnace*, in which the sea offers neither direction nor possibility. In "Cape Dread," for instance, there is no passage at sea; after shipwreck and loss of life, surviving mariners return, chastised by their experience: "We have not gone there again, / Nor ventured ever so far again." What the sea does hold in many poems is a terrifying force of change having nothing to do with "new creation" or renewal. It appears as a deceptive antagonist quickly distorting human markers—the foghorns and buoys through which directions are established. "Sailor Ashore" expresses the notion that the sea-reality is a threatening and deceptive flux, a mere temporal process from which there is no relief.

A note of disillusionment is heard directly in Merwin's "The Bones," in which he appears as a contemporary man on a barren beach. Here he observes "All kinds / Of objects" washed in by the sea and tries to divine their true significance. This project seems dubious from the opening lines, however, as Merwin expresses uncertainty about the eternal song or voice of Creation. "It takes a long time to hear what the sands / Seem to be saying," he confesses: "And then you cannot put it in words nor tell / Why these things should have a voice." Considering the shells on the beach, Merwin admits that "for years" he had not recognized them for what they literally are—the bones of fish. Rather he had seen them as symbols, as vessels of the Creation's song, because after the fish died one could hear seasounds in them. Merwin admits in the poem that, when death occurs and breath ends, "the tune did not / Go on." Revealing lack of confidence in love's triumph over death and in his aesthetics based on this myth, he concludes that the bones of fish littering the beach mean only what they visibly signify: death. "The rest was bones, whatever / Tunes they made."

The signs of death brought in by the sea in "The Bones" include a wrecked ship half-buried in the sand. With "chewed-off / Timbers like the ribs of a man," the ship is a possible portent for the human spirit and the possibility of idealism. Yet to Merwin it communicates no such meaning, and he concludes that, like the shells, it is merely bone— the bones of "man's endeavors." Near the end of the poem he shapes a question expressing uncertainty about human destiny—a question that presages his attention to history in poems of *The Drunk in the Furnace* not explicitly set at sea. "Shells were to shut out the sea," he reasons, and

> The bones of birds were built for floating
> On air and water, and those of fish were devised
> For their feeding depths, while a man's bones were framed
> For what? . . . (217)

## II. A MYTH OF HISTORY

In the late 1950s and in the 1960s Merwin became engaged in actual historical conditions. Returning periodically to America, he worked as a reporter and book reviewer for *The Nation*, writing review-articles that demonstrate an interest in such subjects as social conditions in nineteenth-century Russia. At the same time Merwin focused his poetry on the American scene—a focus evident in the rural imagery of *The Drunk in the Furnace* and in the cityscapes of *The Moving Target*. Further, poems about his ancestors suggest an effort to understand himself in terms of history. Engagement was typical of Western letters in the 1960s as writers became involved with political issues not considered the province of art in modernist aesthetics. Postmodernist poets such as Allen Ginsberg expressed ideological views directly, and by implication claimed that political involvement was the writer's responsibility.

Yet Merwin's approach to historical conditions was rarely literal or directly ideological. By searching out archetypal historical patterns and by continuing to understand history in terms of mythic stories, he adapted historical circumstances to what he terms the "conditions of mythology." Merwin may have developed this approach as he translated the medieval folk epics *The Song of Roland* and *Poem of the Cid*, from 1956 to 1963. In his lengthy introduction to *The Song of Roland*, he reveals his interest in the way that both myth and poetry are created from historical fact. As Charlemagne's nephew who died defending France, the historical figure of Roland was transfigured by popular poets into a mythic hero; a moral type for the Frenchman, he then exerted influence on subsequent French history. In this mythicizing process, Merwin understands that the mythopoeic imagination is archetypal. It seizes the essence of character or scene, eliminating the less relevant details and portraying a typal situation that embodies all particular realities. In the poems of *The Drunk in the Furnace* Merwin creates myths in this manner to express the ethos of rural America. Of the central character in the title poem of the book, he asserts, "All I was trying to do was invent a human being who was not actual but who typified the place. . . . this means that one has made a small myth of the place."[1]

In *The Moving Target* and in *The Lice* (1967), Merwin amplifies the process of mythification. Rather than inventing myths for rural America, he eliminates details of place to a further degree and creates a universal myth for humankind in the modern historical moment. In so doing, Merwin deletes for the most part the traditional narrative structure of myths, even as he retains mythic images, symbols, and postures. Moving toward the essence of the mythmaking role, he places himself at the center of the poem, speaking in the first person. In those poems written from a sense of encounter in the sociohistorical world, Merwin assumes the identity of an anonymous everyman; appearing on the stage of modern history, he tells his own story of humankind.

In Merwin's story the modern world is fallen away from an ideal perfection. He uses the concept of the Fall—one indigenous to many of the world's mythologies—to express modern humankind's inability to conceive of itself as a part of a hierarchichal world of value: fallen human beings no longer understand that they exist in a web of life. The motif of a fall away from this perspective appears in *The Drunk in the Furnace*, *The Moving Target*, and *The Lice*. It is expressed in narrative form in the former volume by "Fable," a poem beginning with the image of a man "Hanging from the top branch of a high tree / With his grip weakening gradually." The tree is obviously the Tree of Life, a symbol from pantheistic mythology, and as the man hangs "With his face toward heaven," it seems that his is an effort to believe the Creation's ideal dimension. Another man, a "passer-by" representing modern béhavior, convinces the climber to let

1. Frank McShane, "A Portrait of W. S. Merwin," *Shenandoah* 21 (1970):12–13.

go because "the tree is falling." When he does let go and falls, he is instantly killed, and the passer-by reacts with cruel indifference by telling the dead body, "All you lacked was a good reason." Concerning both human cruelty and scorn for mythological perspectives, the fable prefigures Merwin's inability to discover meaning in modern history. There is clearly an ominous overtone in his statement when the climber lets go of the tree: "No creature could have survived that fall."

In Merwin's conception of history the reasons for humankind's fall are pride and self-appointment. Such reasoning suggests an indubitable Christian emphasis informing his entire career; yet Merwin is critical of Christianity as a mythology contributing to humankind's bogus self-pride. Christianity separates humankind from nature by attributing to it an unwarranted preeminence: in the mythic injunction in Genesis, God gives Adam dominion over the rest of Creation, as Merwin relates in his review-article "On the Bestial Floor" (313). In the poetry of *The Drunk in the Furnace* Merwin portrays America as a Protestant culture in which this injunction is taken too literally. The effect is smugness, self-righteousness, complacency—a Puritanical behavior—that characterizes the disparate figures portrayed in such poems as "Luther," "Grandmother Dying," and "The Drunk in the Furnace." In "Luther," for instance, Merwin captures the tendency of the Protestant mind to codify reality into dogma, reducing its complexity to a single, simple scheme. The poem is a dramatic monologue in which the great reformer pompously reasons that he, rather than "Holy Church," is an authority at naming evil. Referring to the famed event in which he saw and threw ink at the devil, Luther utters the words through which Merwin discredits the presumptiveness of Protestant orthodoxy. "And every man may know the devil / From this day forth," he claims, "for the devil / Is black. He is black. I have made him so."

Behind Luther's dogmatism, Merwin suggests a fear of experience. By portraying the world as an occasion for sin—as temptation and distraction—orthodox Christianity, in Merwin's understanding, posits inherent evil in Creation. This leads human beings to ignore the possibilities of experience—"A world's unknown dimension." Human characters in *The Drunk in the Furnace* appear little and mean as they consistently retreat from undefined realities. "Pool Room in the Lions' Club" portrays presumably civic-minded men who play pool every day for hours, "year after year." To engage in this "harmless pastime," they retreat to a dim room—"Where the real dark can never come." In "Grandmother Dying" Merwin also reveals that both alienation from nature and moral complacency define the Christian viewpoint. Representing his grandmother as the embodiment of Puritanism, he describes her as one

> Who for ninety-three years,
> Keeping the faith, believed you could get
> Through the strait gate and the needle's eye if
> You made up your mind straight and narrow, kept
> The thread tight and, deaf both to left and to right
> To the sly music beyond the ditches, beat
> Time on the book as you went . . . (249)

Merwin develops his story of humankind in the 1960s as one in which modern humanity rejects all myth, including Christianity. In "On the Bestial Floor," he indicates that Western peoples live in a post-Christian world, utterly without myth in any traditional sense of the term. Instead humankind devises its own myths—conceptions of self and reality—in which humanity is set apart from Creation absolutely by virtue of its intelligence (313). Through reason, expressed as science and technology, humankind triumphs over nature, and in consequence forgets its relationship to that nature. Reason leads humankind, in Merwin's myth, to deify itself: to consider the modern moment as the apex of human development and as the end of the historical process. Merwin has compared the modern era to the Age of Reason because of the common assumption that humanity has realized all its historical ideals (*Products*, 23). In this condition of egoism humankind in Western culture has no feeling nor allegiance to any reality beyond itself.

Separation from the Creation leads to exploitation of Creation in Merwin's historical myth. Possessiveness and destructiveness follow from the condition of egoism because the natural world is regarded as a function of the human will. In a seminal essay titled "Notes for a Preface" (1966), Merwin describes modern humankind as a being who manipulates the Creation, justifying the action by a myth of its own devising: "We exist in an era dedicated to the myth that the biology of the planet . . . can be forced to adapt infinitely to the appetites of one species, organized and deified under the name of economics" (271). For Merwin this modern myth is one of arrogance: Humankind sets itself apart as a god and arrogates the rights of a creator in a world it did not create. The subject of humankind's arrogant destructiveness recurs in a 1982 interview in which Merwin discusses American history as a record of expansionism, declaring that he thinks of it in terms of two Western myths: "One of them the myth of Orpheus obviously—the important thing there is that Orpheus is singing with the animals all around him listening. . . . the other myth is the myth of Phaethon, who says 'Daddy I want to drive these horses,' and ends up in a holocaust."[2] In the latter myth Merwin refers to the Greek tale in which Apollo permitted his son, Phaethon, to drive the chariot bearing the sun. Ignoring limits set by his father, Phaethon drove too close to the earth, causing havoc and destroying himself. Merwin applies the myth to modern humankind, which overruns natural limits, despoils the earth, and demonstrates what he terms "specietal chauvinism."[3]

"The Last One," in *The Lice*, is Merwin's account of humankind's destructiveness toward Creation. It is a tale ironically reversing the Christian story of Genesis in which God created the world in six days. In Merwin's story human

2. Ed Folsom and Cary Nelson, "'Fact Has Two Faces': An Interview with W. S. Merwin," *Iowa Review* 13 (1982):38.
3. Ibid., 31.

beings assume godlike prerogatives and seek to decreate the world by "cutting everything." With a satiric tone recalling the mythlike poems of Edwin Muir, Merwin captures humankind's gratuitous, self-centered logic in deeming itself omnipotent:

> Well they'd made up their minds to be everywhere because
>    why not.
> Everywhere was theirs because they thought so.
> They with two leaves they whom the birds despise.
> In the middle of stones they made up their minds.
> They started to cut. (10)

After all their cutting on the first day, the human beings find "there was one left standing," and they decide to cut it the next day. This last one is not named in the poem in a mythicizing technique through which Merwin suggests that it could be the last living thing of any kind. Yet it should be understood as a tree: it has branches, and it is to be used "for burning." Ultimately it is the Tree of Life, a mythical symbol brought forward from earlier poems such as "Fable."

As Merwin narrates "The Last One," he amplifies the poem's drama: when the last tree is cut its shadow remains on the water beside which it had grown. Uncomfortable with this final visible trace of the last one, "they started trying to get the shadow away." Gradually the humans grow obsessed with effacing the shadow, yet it cannot be obliterated or eradicated: "They laid boards on it the shadow came out on top. / They shone lights on it the shadow got blacker and clearer." A mythic symbol, the shadow signifies the dimension of the natural world transcending physical laws and the activity of humankind. By portraying it as an ineradicable absence, Merwin intimates that the universe is alive with meaning despite humankind's inability to perceive it. As the poem concludes, it is no longer possible to ignore the shadow, for it becomes a kind of pestilence exacting retribution: "It got into eyes the eyes went blind. / The ones that fell down it grew over and they vanished."

In "The Last One" the Creation reasserts its transcendent significance and imposes on egoistic humankind the perennial limitations that constitute life as a creature. However, Merwin sometimes imagines total catastrophe in his story of humanity, indicating that they who "cut everything" might succeed in their destructiveness. In "Notes for a Preface" he maintains that by manipulating the natural world according to its need for comfort humankind might be able to create an artificial environment. It would then find itself adapting to unnatural "man-made circumstances"—an event that would threaten the course of human evolution. "One of the vexed points of modern biology is precisely the definition of a species," Merwin claims, "and the point at which adaptation to changed circumstances requires a new definition for a species that has been transformed into something entirely new" (271). In a simulated environment humankind loses uniquely human status. Freed of the struggle for survival that guaranteed interaction with the natural world, modern humankind is unable to sensuously apprehend reality and to define itself in relation to it. In consequence such human virtues as self-knowledge and self-control, which are based on awareness of natural limitations, are no longer cultivated.

In *The Lice*, "The Finding of Reasons" expresses humankind's dire historical situation. Through images Merwin conveys the modern landscape as one without natural form; it is a world in which there is no continuity either with the human past or with the natural world. "Every memory is abandoned" in Merwin's account: "Even Pain / That is a god to the senses / Can be forgotten." Having gained mastery over nature through technological methods or "uses," human beings have betrayed themselves for they have lost self-mastery. They appear in the poem as unable to control their bodily members: no longer will the feet come "Of themselves freely / To us / Their forgotten masters." That this loss of self-mastery means a loss of historical direction emerges in the final stanza. Merwin imagines that despite human pronouncements of triumph over Creation, and despite the egoistic reasoning that justifies such pronouncements, modern humankind's success is hollow for it has endangered the course of evolution.

> To listen to the announcements you would think
> The triumph
> Were ours
> As the string of the great kite Sapiens
> Cuts our palms
> Along predestined places
> Leaving us
> Leaving
> While we find reasons. (74–75)

Because he has no hope for the historical future, Merwin imagines the present as an irremedial catastrophe. It is a fall toward the end, a process of dying; as one commentator, Harvey Gross, asserts of Merwin's historical viewpoint, "The world at the end of history is a dead world."[4] Merwin often describes the present in images suggesting the mythical apocalypse: things are falling, broken, ending. In "For the Grave of Posterity," in *The Moving Target*, he depicts the gravestone of a future generation: "This stone that is not here," he declares, "commemorates / the emptiness at the end of / history." Merwin frequently employs imagery of rising water and falling rain to recall the mythical deluge that ended a corrupt historical moment. In *The Lice* images of deathly cold and ice create a sensation of the world's end. "The Moths," for example, begins with the lines:

> It is cold here
> In the steel grass
> At the foot of the invisible statue

---

4. "The Writing on the Void: The Poetry of W. S. Merwin," *Iowa Review* 1 (1970):102.

Made by the incurables and called
Justice. (23)

\* \* \*

"The Moths" reveals another reason for Merwin's loss of confidence in humankind's historical future. Dedication to such historical ideals as justice is a hopeless act—one performed by "incurables." In Merwin's story of humankind injustice prevails: history is a record of the lack of balance among nations and classes of people. The same egoism that leads humans to separate themselves from Creation convinces them that they are superior to their fellows. It leads to nationalism and colonialism: to what Merwin calls cultural chauvinism.[5] Opposition to these historical forces emerges in his review-articles that disapprove of French colonialism in Algeria ("Among the Rats") and of Portuguese intervention in another African nation, Angola ("To Name the Wrong").

Although Merwin understands injustice as an archetypal historical pattern of behavior, he specifically implicates America as the heir to the Western cultural legacy of expansionism. With the preservation of Creation in mind, he became involved in the protest against nuclear armaments in the late 1950s and came to view American intervention in Southeast Asia as a form of colonialism. In opposing totalitarianism America becomes totalitarian itself ("Act of Conscience," 479): it becomes the vast, coercive modern empire imagined in Merwin's "Caesar" in *The Lice*. This view discloses the countercultural basis of Merwin's historical myth. In the 1960s writers and intellectuals revised and "demythologized" American history, insisting that America should not be regarded as a nation with a manifest destiny. Instead it should be viewed as one among many countries and as a nation made up of many cultural traditions, not simply the Anglo-Saxon. This revised understanding of American history accounts for the new movement of internationalism in American letters; in it such

5. Folsom and Nelson, "Fact Has Two Faces," 31.

writers as Merwin and Robert Bly expended much energy translating foreign literatures in the belief that American culture might be enriched by them.[6]

In Merwin's perspective injustice is also prevalent within American society. His myth of history encompasses a tradition of radical populism—a fact that links his poetry not simply with Bly's but also with the works of such poets as Gary Snyder and William Stafford. In this tradition the middle class embodies the nationalistic spirit and profits materially at the expense of the people. The ethos of the middle class is possessiveness and expansionism: its typical person is a busy achiever for whom self-centered activity is the sole mode of life. In "Notes for a Preface" Merwin describes this person as "the consumer, who does not know what he sees, hears, wants, or is afraid of, until the voice of the institution has told him" (270). The middle class forms a huge collectivity that is bureaucratically organized and exerts an overwhelming pressure to conform. In Merwin's story the collectivity fails to recognize nonobjectifiable forms of behavior because it refuses either to reflect or to imagine. Insisting that all identity is social, it exteriorizes and therefore reduces the individual's interior being.

In contrast, the popular element of a nation remains in touch with nature and with the sources of life. Earthy and realistic, the people also believe in the life of imagination; they have the viewpoint that Edwin Muir terms "realistic yet credulous."[7] Less covetous and less materialistic than the middle class, the people want little and are not self-aggrandizing in Merwin's story. A vein of poems in his career draws on this spirit of populism in which the poor appear as the simple "salt of the earth," to use a familiar expression. "In the Heart of Europe" in *Green with Beasts*, "The Dry Stone Mason" in *The Lice*, and "Huckleberry

6. See David Ossman, *The Sullen Art: Interviews by David Ossman with Modern American Poets* (New York: Corinth, 1963), 39.

7. Edwin Muir, *The Estate of Poetry* (Cambridge: Harvard University Press, 1962), p. 58.

Woman" in *The Carrier of Ladders* (1971) are notable examples. Further, in 1961 Merwin studied the American populist revolt of the 1890s, planning a long narrative poem about it; and in his review "The Relevance of Some Russians," he expresses sympathy for nineteenth-century Russian populists who were oppressed by the nobility. Describing the populist movement to resist Czarism, Merwin declares: "The history of the movement is above all a record of individuals . . . faced with confusion and injustice. . . . struggling to create values in a world without them" (184).

The concept of an unjust class conflict explains many of the poems of *The Moving Target* and *The Lice*. Through his first-person persona Merwin takes the side of the people, projecting the struggle of the individual against a vaguely depicted, coercive collectivity. Poems having to do with social existence are based on a pattern of encounter and resistance in which the oppressor may be imagined as "they," a "thug on duty," or an "inspector of stairs," while the speaker appears as a populist hero—or more exactly, as an antihero. In "The Hydra," a poem in *The Lice*, Merwin imagines the collectivity as a mythical monster: it is a many-headed hydra that would fatally reduce the individual. The hydra is made up of the living dead who live only in their names, that is, only by virtue of objectifiable social identity. Relationship with these dead-in-life is impossible, which explains the speaker's assertion as the poem begins: "No no the dead have no brothers." Avoiding collectivity in an effort to preserve individuality, he declares in the second stanza: "The Hydra calls me but I am used to it / It calls me Everybody / But I know my name and do not answer."

"Acclimatization," in *The Moving Target*, portrays the reduction of the individual in grimly humorous images. Sounding much like the populist figures in the dramas of Samuel Beckett, the speaker relates his attempt to "acclimate" or to become involved with society. With naive generosity he has contributed his talents to "them"—his generally depicted antagonists. However, he receives no satisfaction because the collectivity understands his contribution in purely physical terms. Taking more and more from him, they finally deprive him of actual physical being:

> . . . I
> Got hungry, they fed me. I gave them
> My solemn word in payment. And all
> The bells in the city rang in triumph
> Like cash registers. They gave me their credit
> And left me with little hope.
> When I woke I discovered
> That they had taken my legs . . . (15)

At the end of "Acclimatization" the speaker is reduced to a helpless cripple. He appears as a legless man, sitting amid the society while "they / Demand, they demand, / they demand." By asking "What / Do I have that is my own," he suggests that Merwin's myth of a populist antihero is an effort "to create values in a world without them." In contrast to values established by mythic heroes who were society's exemplars, the values postulated in Merwin's story are nonheroic. The first value is simple resistance to the immoral direction of the middle-class collectivity: because in Merwin's perspective the national conscience had atrophied, everyone was responsible for passively resisting such national policies as nuclear armament. Resistance should be enacted with humility in that tradition of peaceful civil dissent established by Henry David Thoreau. It should be committed in what Merwin terms "a spirit of openness" ("Act of Conscience," 465). Openness and openhandedness are major motifs in *The Moving Target*; they are inverse images for the close-fisted possessiveness characterizing puritanical poetic characters. Openness initiates community, and Merwin remains dedicated to such openness—a fact attested by the title of his latest book, *Opening the Hand*.

More vigorous forms of resistance are imagined in several of Merwin's poems. In "The Next" of *The Moving Tar-*

*get*, resistance is expressed as a bold and courageous protest against a conspiracy to deprive the people of their life and limb. Yet in this poem and elsewhere Merwin implies that protest will have little effect on the course of history. For this reason Merwin most often imagines resistance as an act of departure—as simple movement away from the reductive pressure of historical life. Echoing the mythical theme of exploration from Merwin's early poetry, the motif of departure reveals his inability to find justice in any sociohistorical mode of identity. In "Departure's Girl-Friend" he describes an event in which the speaker refuses the identity that society would unjustly impose. Attempting to escape her loneliness as the poem begins, she decides to take a voyage in her boat and walks through the city toward the wharf, carrying a wreath of flowers. At the wharf she encounters the representative of the sociohistorical moment. When he asks where she is going, she tells him with openness that she is going to her boat, and in his response Merwin typifies the society's unwillingness to understand her as she understands herself: "He said, this is the stone wharf, lady, / You don't own anything here." As she turns away and moves on, Merwin insists on the self's right to define itself over and beyond any social definition. "I step once more / Through a hoop of tears and walk on," she says, "holding this / Buoy of flowers in front of my beauty, / Wishing myself the good voyage."

"Departure's Girl-Friend" indicates a reason for the success of Merwin's story of humankind. A poem containing more than one level of meaning, it ultimately expresses Merwin's struggle to survive as a creative artist in the modern world that holds no inspiration for him. The poem discloses an effort to preserve imagination in "the other and hated city"—amid a landscape of technological objects and among a majority of human beings overwhelmingly unsympathetic to poetic imagination. In framing his own sense of rejection, Merwin appealed to a postwar generation that feared that a technological organization of life was the enemy of individuality. This generation came to be guided by the existentialist assumption that there is no justice in any social authority that denies the primacy of self-expression. In this respect the social encounters in Merwin's poetry tell an existentialist's tale.

Ultimately this view toward society is the Romantic one, placing Merwin's poetry in the American tradition of Thoreau and Samuel Clemens. In the tradition of radical innocence, the American Adam moves away from all social convention and prevailing belief. The question arising with regard to this tradition should be applied to Merwin's poetry: is there a "moving target" justifying flight from society? What source of solace outside the self is to be asserted? In a number of poems Merwin indicates as an objective a past mode of belief through which to redeem the present. There is elegiac yearning for this past from which historical man has fallen in Merwin's "Resolution," in *The Moving Target*. The speaker hears a child playing piano music that becomes less audible even as he is threatened by a vague coercive force. Apparently he feels that time is taking him away from inspiriting sources, for he declares near the end of the poem:

> *Oh let it be yesterday surely*
> *It's time.* (68)

# III. RECLAIMING MYTHIC CONSCIOUSNESS

The decade of the 1960s was for Merwin a period of re-evaluation and experimentation. From his farmhouse in southern France he pondered essential poetic principles to counteract catastrophic historical conditions. Merwin was convinced that contemporary art merely reflected those conditions: it revealed the separation of human beings from Creation, describing "the squalid landscapes of a world made and polluted by man alone." In his view art should have "integrated sensuous criteria" ("Notes," 272). It should portray human interaction with the nonhuman world. As he mythicized history in his poems, Merwin moved toward his mature intellectual position that poetry might redeem contemporary conditions by restoring mankind's ancient connection with the natural world.

The first stage in Merwin's restoration is an attempt to dramatize consciousness filled with the world. In the poetry of *The Moving Target*, *The Lice*, and *The Carrier of Ladders*, he presents an immediate awareness of nature that precedes all conscious thought about it. In this preconscious mode of thought the perceiving subject is bound indissolubly to the thing perceived and experiences no sense of distance from it. Merwin believes that this mode of consciousness was extant in the past when mankind used imagination to speak about the world and thereby created myths. The mythic consciousness of premodern people and their manner of speaking about the world become for him a quintessential poetry that he terms "the original idiom" and that he defines as "the great language itself, the vernacular of imagination, that at one time was common to men. It is a tongue that is loosed in the service of immediate recognitions, and that in itself would make it foreign in our period" ("Notes," 269–70).

Merwin's interest in primitive mythic consciousness represents a postmodernist attitude toward myth. A key term

31

in this movement is *simplification*, as poets sought to present experience with greater immediacy. Avoiding ideas and traditional cultural forms, they sought to make their art more real by making it a model of consciousness. In the mythological poems of such modernist poets as Graves, there is discursive treatment of mythic subjects. Identifying with specific mythic figures from the cultural past, the poet retells the experience, comments on its contemporary relevance, and thus reveals the continuity between past and present in mankind's cultural history. But for such poets as Merwin and Ted Hughes this approach to myth lacks intensity: in their poems there is no attempt to identify with specific mythic events or characters from cultural history, nor is there effort to comment on the relevance of the past. From the belief that the contemporary present is hopelessly overrefined, they avoid discursive statement and instead actually seek to dramatize mythic consciousness. This "presentational" approach discloses the primitivism in the postmodern viewpoint: the thought and the art of primitive peoples are considered intrinsically valuable.

For Merwin mythic consciousness of the world results from elimination of the historical mode of awareness. Because it is based upon pragmatic reason, historical consciousness is awareness of the world as a static object—as an entity that can be manipulated through knowledge of laws and formulas. One acquires this knowledge through the process of education; at the same time, one is socialized to regard objects as having a certain value established by convention. In Merwin's understanding, therefore, the educated person perceives the world in terms of his relationship to other people. Socialization establishes distance not merely from the world but also from one's inward or preconscious experience of it. Diluting experience, it promotes a self-image in which success depends on one's ability to manipulate the world.

Such poems of *The Lice* as "The Child" and "Peasant" reveal movement away from historical consciousness in favor of "immediate recognitions" of the world. In "The Child," for instance, the speaker is disillusioned with the course of his life, for he has sought to understand experience through the eyes of others. "Sometimes it is inconceivable that I should be the age I am," he asserts as the poem begins; as it unfolds, he suggests the inadequacy of his previous attitude toward life as a series of objectifiable actions in which he was the principal agent. From this viewpoint progress and satisfaction have eluded him: "I try to remember my faults," he states, "but it is never / Satisfactory the list is never complete." Near the end of the poem it is evident that he would like to avoid this mode of consciousness and to regain awareness of himself in relation to the world. Because mythic awareness is prior to the socialized adult's awareness, Merwin expresses the need for it by using the Romantic metaphor that the child is father to the man:

> While I can I try to repeat what I believe
> Creatures spirits not this posture
> I do not believe in knowledge as we know it
> But I forget
> This silence coming at intervals out of the
>     shell of names
> . . . . . . . . . . . . .
> The child that will lead you. (37–38)

Formally, "The Child" reveals Merwin's effort to mythicize the speaking voice of his poetry. In the movement away from historical consciousness he eliminates the personal details of his existence. Having nothing to do with socialized personality, the "original idiom" is "common to men": therefore Merwin concentrates on the essence of the situation, using generic terms and language and avoiding reference to specific persons, places, or things.[1] For ex-

---

1. See Charles Molesworth, *The Fierce Embrace: A Study of Contemporary American Poetry* (Columbia: University of Missouri Press, 1979), 148.

ample, the speaker of "The Child" indicates a dissatisfaction with age but does not indicate whether he (or she) is thirty or fifty years old. Gender is not indicated, nor does the speaker identify any of the others who have caused self-consciousness. For Merwin the named I belongs to society, in contrast to the real I who is anonymous, presocial identity. This is why he declares, "Silence comes at intervals out of the shell of names"; and in his poetry a motif of names is pervasive. Names and the act of naming are associated with the possessiveness of historical consciousness, while healthful awareness involves penetration to realities behind the names. In dramatizing mythic or generic identity, Merwin hopes to draw the reader more fully into the poem, and thus to nourish his or her consciousness of the world. Because personal details might distract the reader by drawing attention to the personality of the poet, elimination of them enables the reader to participate more fully in the event of the poem.

Mythic consciousness is for Merwin a simplified mode of perception: it is consciousness absorbed entirely in the simplest processes and events of the Creation. The passage of cosmic time, the cycle of the seasons, the alternation of day and night, the rising and waning moon: these are the natural events that appeal to mythic consciousness, and from which it derives delight. To dramatize familiarity with simple events Merwin often uses the technique of personification. In "Evening," a poem in *The Lice*, he appears engaged in a human task—"trying / To finish something"—as the light of day fades. Feeling "something passing," he imagines evening as a presence and identifies the event: "it is only / Evening again the old hat without a head / How long will it be til he speaks when he passes." In a number of poems in the middle of *The Lice*, Merwin appears as a man who takes pleasure in doing such simple things as walking out at night to watch plants grow. In "The Cold Before Moonlight" he dramatizes consciousness so keenly tuned to natural events it hears frost forming on a winter night. That such "immediate recognitions" of nature are desirable yet foreign in the contemporary era is implied in his reaction to this event.

> It is too simple to turn to the sound
> Of frost stirring among its
> Stars like an animal asleep
> . . . . . . . . . . . . . . . . . .
> If there is a place where this is the language may
> It be my country. (46)

These lines also suggest Merwin's intention to convey through mythic consciousness a gratitude for life. For him life is primary, and mythic consciousness is life-affirming. Unlike historical consciousness, it does not take life for granted; rather, it perceives existence-in-the-world as a cause for celebration—as a fact more important than historical action in which life is purposefully organized and directed toward temporal ends.

Merwin's effort to bring consciousness face-to-face with the world is an attempt to call attention to its essential substances. Earth, air, fire, and water are the simple elements that play a predominant role—both as image and as symbol—in the poetry of his later career. These are the natural "Simplicities" mentioned in Merwin's "To Where We Are" in *The Moving Target*: they are the very stuff of the universe— the last things that a simplified consciousness could recognize. By calling attention to simple elements Merwin expresses the way in which human life depends on them and is even composed from them. For him psychic health consists of this recognition, which is also an awareness of one's dependence on Creation. One must realize, for instance, that water is a simple necessity; this is the meaning of Merwin's actions in his poem "Vocations," in *The Moving Target*. Obviously concerned with aesthetic practice, the poem depicts a man who yearns all day for "Simplicity" and tempts it with "clear water." At the end of the poem he gets up "To wash my shadow in the river," and ends by proclaiming: "In a direction that was lost / The hands of the water have found tomorrow."

Through imagery of air, fire, and water, Merwin also evokes the endlessness of cosmic time in comparison to the brief centuries of human history. He captures the sense in which these elemental substances were the first things. To go further, he characterizes them as the indivisible essence of all that visibly appears. In so doing Merwin takes inspiration from Greek pre-Socratic philosophers—from thinkers such as Heraclitus, whose anecdote about Homer is the epigraph for *The Lice*. These pantheistic philosophers each selected an element to characterize the unchanging unity behind visible change. For Thales, the element was water; for Anaximenes, it was air; for Heraclitus, the life of the universe was an everliving fire into which things flamed forth into being before dying out. Merwin uses these elements as mythic symbols repeatedly in later poems in order to signify the eternal life of the Creation. In "The Well," in *The Carrier of Ladders*, he describes water as "the immortal" to which everything and everyone must come:

> Under the stone sky the water
> waits
> with all its songs inside it
> . . . . . . . . . . . . . . . .
> the days
> walk across the stone in heaven
> unseen as planets at noon
> while the water
> watches the same night. (37)

Merwin also identifies directly with air, fire, or water to communicate mythic consciousness of the world. The eternal and necessary properties of these elements so captivate his imagination that they become metaphors for existence, as he describes his life in terms of them. Because air is penetrated by natural events and objects, it becomes an analogue for the simple consciousness that is touched by the world in Merwin's "Air," in *The Moving Target*. "I remember the rain with its bundle of roads," Merwin proclaims: "I remember the leaves sitting in judgement." By declaring that he goes "this way" and then "that way," the speaker also identifies with the random direction of air, and toward the poem's conclusion he describes his existence as ageless and placeless—as unencumbered by historical time or circumstance. "Young as I am, old as I am," he asserts: "I forget tomorrow, the blind man."

In "Air" Merwin's effort to simplify consciousness leads him to an obviously fictive poetic identity. In contrast to poems in *The Lice* in which he appears as a simple man wondering at natural events, in "Air" the mythification of identity is more severe. In *The Carrier of Ladders* Merwin redoubles his effort to present mythic consciousness filled with the world. As in the poems of Theodore Roethke, poetic consciousness appears utterly caught up with things: perception of natural events and landscapes is so immediate that consciousness is articulated by means of them— even more literally than in "Air." Such poems as "Not These Hills" and "Snowfall" reveal a more evident blurring of the boundaries of human identity and of nature. "Snowfall" seems to be about Merwin's mother, for it is dedicated to her. Its opening lines suggest the poet's sense of accomplishment with his aesthetic vocation; then he relates that in the night the "silent kin" he loved as a child have arrived to remind him of his past. This consciousness of his past as a human being is stated in terms of the snow that has also fallen during the night:

> I eat from the hands
> of what for years have been junipers
> the taste has not changed
> I am beginning
> . . . . . . . . . . .
> and in the sunlight snow drops from branches
> leaving its name in the air
> and a single footprint
>
> brother. (69)

These lines reveal an almost total obliteration of social identity. The image of the snow as a "brother," for instance, demonstrates Merwin's tendency to substitute community with the natural world for human community. This substitution is made complete by the poem's language, which makes it hard to determine meaning. There is an almost total lack of prose discursiveness: so intent is Merwin on recapturing the "original idiom" that, as he faces the world, he forgets the logic of human speech. Refusing to appear as a civilized "man speaking to men," he absorbs fully the mode of primitive art in which speech is a chantlike voice— the "lyric cry of emotion" that Joyce cited as existing prior to dramatic modes of art. In this mode the poet projects a mythical, transhistorical identity that can go anywhere and do anything. This mode marks such poems of *The Carrier of Ladders* as "Psalm: Our Fathers" and "Lark." It is evident in the opening line of "The Wave" in *The Lice*: "I inhabited the wake of a long wave." Such lines ought to be compared to those in *The Song of Amergin*, an ancient Celtic poem, in which the speaker chants: "I am a flood: across a plain / I am a wind: on a deep lake." [2]

Because Merwin does not appear in his poems as a social being, his commentators have not always received his work favorably. At midcareer utter concentration on the world is achieved at the expense of the human world with its complicated ethical questions. Thus one of Merwin's commentators derides "his starved and mute stance"; another demands more "poems that situate us in the world or elaborate on real conditions." [3] This response to Merwin's mythic identity represents a vein of criticism that began in a 1961 review in which fellow poet James Dickey asked that

2. Robert Graves, *The White Goddess: A Historical Grammar of Poetic Myth* (New York: Farrar, 1966), 13.

3. Helen Vendler, *Part Nature: Part Us: Modern American Poets* (Cambridge: Harvard University Press, 1980), 233; James Atlas, "Diminishing Returns: The Writings of W. S. Merwin," in *American Poetry since 1960: Some Critical Perspectives*, ed. Robert B. Shaw, (Chatham, Eng.: MacKay, 1973), 79.

Merwin "suffer a little at the hands of his subjects."[4] The criticism is justified, especially in the sense in which poetry is a *magister vitae*, to use Matthew Arnold's phrase. Historically, poetry has focused on actions in a human world—on such specifically human virtues as loyalty or courage. For Merwin, however, poetry is primarily a matter of perception or of "seeing." In a 1982 interview he professes inability to take inspiration from historical circumstances or to write discursive poetry in that branch of the postmodernist tradition associated with Whitman and William Carlos Williams. Instead Merwin cites the importance of writers like Thoreau, echoing his earlier commitment to an art of "immediate recognitions." He explains that in Thoreau's work the world is exalted: the reader is able to see it as "completely alive."[5] Like his early work, Merwin's later poetry is designed to inculcate wonder. The dicta of Wallace Stevens is perennially true for him. "A poem," Stevens claims, "should stimulate some sense of living and of being alive."[6]

Merwin's "In the Time of the Blossoms" in *The Carrier of Ladders* illustrates his intention to present a vitalizing view of the world. In the poem he appears with consciousness filled by the world, and he speaks directly to it so that the form of direct address imparts a feeling of the world's value. The subject of the poem is an ash tree that is about to bloom in springtime; as the speaker faces the tree, he begs to hear the music that seems to be playing in its branches. "Ash tree," he declares,

> all over you leaf skeletons
> fine as sparrow bones
> stream out motionless
> on white heaven

4. "The Death and Keys of the Censor," *Sewanee Review* 69 (1961):328.

5. Ed Folsom and Cary Nelson, "'Fact Has Two Faces': An Interview with W. S. Merwin," *Iowa Review* 13 (1982):34.

6. *Opus Posthumous,* edited with an introduction by Samuel French Morse (New York: Knopf, 1966), 177.

staves of one
unbreathed music
Sing to me. (138)

\*   \*   \*

"In the Time of the Blossoms" reveals that for Merwin mythic consciousness is awareness of the world's creative principle. The "one / unbreathed music" playing in the ash tree's branches is the spiritual force turning the world—the unheard music of cosmic unity. Through *The Moving Target*, *The Lice*, and *The Carrier of Ladders*, Merwin recovers his belief in this creative principle that he imagined in his early poetry as a myth of love. On several occasions in his later career he identifies poetry with consciousness of a spiritual dimension of existence, calling it hope rather than love. In "Notes for a Preface," for instance, Merwin associates poetry and hope, suggesting that they are similar because both transcend an empirical consciousness of life. Using the existentialist concept of hope versus despair, Merwin asserts that no art can result from despair, which is capitulation to the naturalist's view of human life and to the determinism of the historical process. Merwin intimates that, in contrast, poetry and hope depend on recognition of a creative power transcending the closed world of time: "I imagine the writing of a poem . . . still betrays the existence of hope, which is why poetry is more and more chary of the conscious mind, in our age. And what the poem manages to find hope for may be part of what it keeps trying to say" (272).

Conception of a world-creating principle is vital to Merwin's role as a mythmaker, because it enables him to see the present as the locus of invisible forces. As one of two dimensions of existence that he mentions in the 1982 interview, the creative dimension imbues the visible world of fact with another possible meaning.[7] It gives the facts two sides, enabling the poet to reorganize and transform

7. Folsom and Nelson, "Fact Has Two Faces," 43.

40

them—to make fact into myth. For Merwin the world-creating principle is the mysterious source of existence. Transcending human consciousness, it is "A world's unknown dimension"—the *mysterium tremendum* that forms the root of the world's mythologies. This meaning is implied in Merwin's foreword to his translations of the work of Jean Follain, a twentieth-century French poet. Describing Follain's vision, Merwin notices that it is centered on a timeless mystery, "the mystery that stays with us and does not change: the present." That the mystery is creative is implied in Merwin's comment that it makes visible details seem "an evocation of the processions of an immeasurable continuum" (vii).

Consciousness of the mysterious creative principle is awareness that the world is evolving, turning forward to complete itself dynamically like a gigantic organism. In Merwin's story the world-creating power brings the present to birth, literally causing it to "appear" or to "be" out of darkness and nonbeing. Phenomenon in Merwin's later poetry comes to light across the ground of cosmic time and life that is an abyss of spirit, freedom, nothing. In fact nothing is a motif in Merwin's poetry: like silence it is an eternal background for what appears, as in these lines from "Not These Hills" in *The Carrier of Ladders*:

> spring here
> I am shown to me
> as flies waking in the south walls
> emerging from darkness one
> at a time
> dark
> then gone
> with nothing between them
> but the sun. (27)

The myth of creation founded on an abyss of spirit and nonbeing is one that Merwin may have developed through contact with Greek philosophers. Possibly it derives directly from the writing of Nicolas Berdyaev, a twentieth-century Russian philosopher who was also influenced by the Greeks and whom Merwin read at this point in his career. For Berdyaev the creating principle is the numinous world or Ungrund—a fiery chaotic mass of elemental possibility. For Merwin, as for Berdyaev, this final principle of life is a mysterious paradox: it is at once both everything and nothing. Merwin indicates that this paradoxical creating principle is the source of existence in a line in "Shaving without a Mirror," in *Opening the Hand*: "nothing is native of fire and everything is born of it," he declares. The paradoxical emphases implicit in Merwin's myth have caused confusion among his commentators, some of whom claim that Merwin is a poet of darkness, one preoccupied with absence or nonbeing. They stress that things disappear in his poetry, as in the lines above from "Not These Hills."[8] Others find Merwin an affirmative poet, discerning presence or immanence. They discover in his work a fullness of being, citing his focus on a present that realizes all possibilities of being.[9]

Merwin often symbolizes the world-creating power as a mythical river or current of spiritual energy. In "Huckleberry Woman," in *The Carrier of Ladders*, it is a "black stream" making the poet aware of loss and grieving; in "The Current," in *Writings to an Unfinished Accompaniment*, it suffuses the world and makes it appealing. Merwin's "On the Mountain" in *The Compass Flower* explicitly describes an invisible river impelling the world and bringing the present into being. The poet appears on a mountain at dawn as the wind in a pine tree causes awareness of an

> air river too deep to be seen
> current with no surface
> then can be heard and felt
> it carries deep reflections of birds
> and of sunrise clouds
> thoughts into the sea of day. (19)

8. See Richard Howard, "A Poetry of Darkness," *The Nation* 14 (December 1970):634.

9. Jarold Ramsey, "The Continuities of W. S. Merwin: 'What Has Escaped Us, We Bring with Us,'" *Massachusetts Review* 14 (1973):588.

Merwin's "Lackawanna" in *The Carrier of Ladders* is the most complete expression of the creative principle as a river of spiritual life. In this poem Merwin seems to face an actual river—the Lackawanna River that flowed past his boyhood home in Pennsylvania. He recollects his experience of the river as the poem unfolds, remembering running on girders of its bridges and the warnings with which adults caution young boys about rivers. Yet it is evident that the river represents the world's huge indwelling power. Like the "immeasurable continuum," it contains all darkness and spirit; thus to the poet it calls to mind "terror / a truth." Addressing it, he declares, "you flowed from under / and through the night the dead drifted down you / all the dead." Consciousness of this spiritual current in the world is awareness that one exists in an awful mystery, for one recognizes that one's own life is sustained and embraced by it. This recognition is heard in the poem's opening lines. "Where you begin / in me / I have never seen," Merwin claims, "but I believe it now / rising dark / but clear."

"Lackawanna" also suggests the importance of the world-creating principle in Merwin's aesthetic. The poem implies that, through rules and regulations, other human beings have impeded the poet's access to the spiritual life symbolized by the river. In the poem's final lines there is a figurative baptism as the speaker abolishes all distance between himself and the world by setting foot in the river. As he does so he refers to it as the biblical river Jordan, claiming

> told to be afraid
> I wake black to the knees
> so it has happened
> I have set foot in you
> both feet
> Jordan
> too long I was ashamed
> at a distance. (45)

The note of aspiration and ecstasy heard in these lines informs *The Carrier of Ladders*. The poems in this book form a series in Merwin's quest for inspiration—for the creative impulse inspired by conception of the world-creating principle. Consciousness of it causes renewal of perception: each time it is conceived the visible world appears to be beginning. The thirst for renewal is one of the "conditions of mythology," for mythic consciousness resists historical awareness in an attempt to return to its sense of the way things were at the beginning. In the time of the beginning, the burdensome progression of chronological time ceases to bear one down; there is a sensation of the primordial unity of all created things.[10]

Renewal of consciousness is a critical act for Merwin, because in an art that would restore the world there must be perpetually fresh perspective. Every creative act should depict a new creation: in the words of Berdyaev, a creative act "makes a new plan for existence" by duplicating the original act of creation in which the world began.[11] For this reason "the beginning" is a dominant mythic motif in Merwin's art from *The Moving Target* through *The Carrier of Ladders*. The beginning is his image for the mythical moment in which both man and world were created together—without separation or distance between them. For Merwin art recaptures this moment when the artist perceives his unity with the world and is able to articulate it. Furthermore, in the mythical moment of art, the artist grasps the sense in which he has eternal life in the life of the Creation. Through imagination he exists before time; identifying with the world's creating power, he asserts that what is visibly before him exists by virtue of an eternal process. That the moment of art is an eternal moment explains the often enigmatic declarations of such poems from *The Carrier of Ladders* as "The Birds on the Morning of Going." Listening to bird-song causes Merwin to conceive the eternal song of life in the world, and therefore he declares: "If I can say yes I / must say it to this."

10. Mircea Eliade, *The Myth of the Eternal Return: Or, Cosmos and History*, trans. Willard R. Trask (Princeton: Princeton University Press, 1965), 86.
11. *The Beginning and the End*, trans. R. M. French (New York: Harper, 1957), 185.

In "The Piper" from *The Carrier of Ladders* Merwin personifies the beginning, revealing that creativity is perpetual renewal. The poem concerns his career as an artist, since in it he reflects on his early poetic effort in relation to his current viewpoint. He recalls studying laboriously twenty years before in the attic of a house in a foreign country, and he asserts that he was not only high above the ground but also "high above the piper"—an image for the source of his creativity. "I was older then / than I ever hope to be again," he declares, because despite the advance of the years he realizes that poetry is a perpetually reborn awareness of the world. To hear the piper requires repeated eschewal of historical consciousness and continual return to the mysterious source of life in the present. In the concluding lines he yearns for one more vision of the world as it appeared in the mythical moment in which it began: "Beginning / I am here," he proclaims; "please / be ready to teach me."

Through the implication of the title "The Piper," Merwin asserts his identity as a singer, as an Orphic poet. The son of the Muse Calliope, Orpheus sang of the world's beginning and of the origin of all things. In Orphic thought deriving from ancient Asian mythology and infusing Platonic myth, the transcendent creating principle was the One out of which all things were created in a process that involved separation from the One. It is this One of which Merwin sings in "Gift" in *Writings to an Unfinished Accompaniment*. Referring to it without symbol or metaphor, Merwin identifies it as an impersonal pantheistic force in the poem's first three stanzas. He asserts that it was given to him as one of "the gifts of unknown" and that he must be led by it, "as streams are led by it / and braiding flights of birds." Brooding on its mystery as a transcendent principle, he wonders: "what does it not hope knowing itself no child of time." In the final stanza Merwin invokes the creating principle as the One that unifies all being. "I call to it Nameless One O Invisible / Untouchable Free," and he begs it: "live with me / be my eyes / my tongue and my hands."

Through such lines Merwin reveals that the world-creating power is one with his own creative gift. It is the basis of his identity as a poet speaking to a reader; it is both source and substance of what he would communicate. Therefore he invokes the One in the final line of "Gift": "come and be given." Merwin continues his effort to give to the reader mythic consciousness of the world in his later poetry. Yet he dramatizes this consciousness less and less frequently. Instead he speaks more directly to the reader, seeking to impart an understanding of how the actual present may be viewed as a perpetually new, original world.

# IV. The Myth of an Original World

In *The Carrier of Ladders*, in *Writings to an Unfinished Accompaniment*, and in *The Compass Flower*, Merwin tells the story of an original world. This is the first, paradisiacal world yearned for in all mythologies—the world of the beginning from which mankind has not yet fallen. Concentrating on the attributes and qualities of this world, Merwin tells tales, anecdotes, proverbs, and sayings, rendering the world intelligible in an increasingly descriptive poetic mode. His effort to make the mythical world appear in his poetry corresponds to his writing of prose-poems and prose fiction in the 1970s. *The Miner's Pale Children*, a book of stories and prose parables, was published simultaneously with *The Carrier of Ladders* in 1971; *Houses and Travellers*, a similar work in prose, accompanied *The Compass Flower* in 1977. Like Yeats in *A Vision*, Merwin turns to prose as a medium of clarification, exploring the subjects and the symbols that appear in his poetry.

Merwin's story of an original world represents a culmination of his effort to restore awareness of nature. In telling the story, he realizes his role as a mythmaker, for his poems take on the etiological function of myth: they explain for the reader by means of imagination how the present came into being. Creatively transfiguring appearances, Merwin tells the reader how the world could be seen—if only the reader would open his eyes and ears. A good example is Merwin's "Under Black Leaves" in *Writings to an Unfinished Accompaniment*, in which he would help the reader understand that he is situated in a present mysteriously connected to the eternal design of Creation. Merwin appears in the poem on an autumn night, looking through the window at the moon and stars and listening to the song of crickets. He imagines that this song derives from a primordial event occurring long before human history; and he connects the two events by telling a tale:

>     certain stars leaving their doorways
>     hoped to become crickets
>     these soon to fall even threw
>     dice for the months
>
>     . . . . . . . . . . . . .
>
>     that game was long before men
>     but the sounds travelled slowly
>     only now a few
>     arrive in the black trees
>     on the first night of autumn. (56)

The outline of Merwin's story of the world is the ancient Asian myth in which heaven and earth existed side by side before the primordial rupture or Fall. In this version of the paradise myth, heaven closely resembles the earth; it is an extraterrestrial earth—a perfect, archetypal world. After the Fall there is distance between heaven and earth, but the means of communication still exists through passage up certain mountains or trees. This account of Creation and the Fall also occurs in tales of American Indians that Merwin studied and transcribed at this point in his career. For the Indians this world evolved from others in which mankind had easy access to gods and animals; in fact, the ground of this world, for the Indian, was the ceiling of a subterranean world—a concept Merwin uses quite literally in his poem "Dreamers" in *Writings to an Unfinished Accompaniment*. Merwin was drawn to Indian mythology because in it human vision is an inward imaginative faculty that perceives appearances as the temporalization of eternal forces. His debt to primitive myths and tales in general is apparent in the title *The Carrier of Ladders*, for the phrase is taken from a West African tribal song in which the bearer of the dead tells the carrier of ladders, "It is the day of trouble."

A dominant characteristic of Merwin's mythical world is its unity or oneness. Each thing exists as an archetype; there is only one of everything. At the same time all things are unified by the world-creating power in each of them, rendering each indivisible from the whole. In Merwin's story the great sin is division—an act in which mankind separates things from the fabric of being and subjects them to particular uses. Division is for Merwin a category of human reason. It is the tendency to compare, contrast, and define, and it causes humankind to live in the historical realm, which is fallen, jaded, copied. In "Lantern," in *Writings to an Unfinished Accompaniment*, Merwin reveals that in the original world nothing can be divided or broken. Referring specifically to his world as "A little way ahead," he describes it as an archetypal place in which each thing is filled with the spiritual life,

> for in that world nothing can break
> so no one believes in the plural there
> . . . . . . . . . . . . . . . . . . . . . . .
> that is the place of a god
> for a god is alone
> he sits on each different leaf
> he holds in each eye
> differently
> in each hand differently. (77)

The presence of spiritual life in the things of the world makes them interrelated and interchangeable. In Merwin's story everything communicates with everything else, and so becomes capable of exchange. Emphasizing the principle that all exists mysteriously in the one web of Creation, Merwin the mythmaker becomes a magician who finds analogies and correspondences between all living things. In "The Horse," for instance, a poem in *The Compass Flower*, Merwin envisions the stream of life that is in both creatures and plants. Because he imagines that a dead tree once tossed its branches as a horse tosses its head, he is able to declare as the poem opens, "In a dead tree / there is the ghost of a horse." In the first world of Merwin's poems there is also community of events. Both cosmic and human events occur simultaneously and can be exchanged. Using the concept of human lives as interchangeable, Merwin combats selfish individualism in such poems as "On the Silent Anniversary of a Reunion" in *Writings to an Unfinished Accompaniment*. "Each of these hours has been to you first," he declares: "and stared / and forgotten / but I know the burnt smell."

In such poems of *Finding the Islands* as "In the Red Mountain," Merwin stresses the simultaneity of cosmic events. Without comment, he describes them in terms of one another, for his intention is to place the reader at the center of the original world:

> Leaves still on branches
> turn at night into
> first snow
> . . . . . . .
> Many times clouds were mountains
> then one morning mountains
> woke as clouds. (19)

In Merwin's story the original world is transparent: it can be looked through. With this motif Merwin expresses the need for imagination to penetrate the surface appearances and to see into the creative, celestial dimension. Because it touches on this dimension of pure potentiality, each thing has an inward possibility that does not appear until it is grasped by imagination. Merwin develops this chapter of his story through imagery of doors and windows: a transparent world and everything in it have doors and windows to which the key is imagination. Perhaps the best expression of this concept is Merwin's "To the Hand," in *Writings to an Unfinished Accompaniment*. In this poem he describes the original world, stating that in it "for every real lock / there is only one key." The key, he claims, is "invisible" because it is imagination, and as he develops the tale it is clear that imagination opens the door to an understanding of the spiritual dimension of the world—which he expresses as the mythical river. "It's the key to the one real door," he claims: "It opens the water and the sky both at once / It's already in the downward river." Concluding the poem,

Merwin urges himself and the reader to turn the key and "open the river."

Through the mythic symbol of doors Merwin also represents the creative function. As mythmaker, he is doorlike: his office is to provide entry for the reader into the original world. Mythification of poetic identity in terms of doors and doorways is a prevalent motif in all Merwin's later poetry. Because through him the reader hears the eternal song of life, Merwin declares in a poem in *The Lice*: "Let me kneel in the doorway empty except for the song." In a later poem, "Apples," in *The Compass Flower*, Merwin portrays himself as one who awakens beside a pile of keys. From all the keys, it is his task to find the one that unlocks the significance of the present: "The one / to the door of a cold morning."

Even phenomenal objects have inward life and existence in Merwin's transparent world. Things that appear lifeless or abandoned belonged somehow to the eternal stream of life before they became fallen into their present human use. By revealing the connection Merwin discloses the history or origins of things: in essence, he tells their story. Such poems of *The Carrier of Ladders* as "Night of Shirts" and "Shoe Repairs" demonstrate this mythic function; in the latter poem a pair of shoes is linked to its origin in the skins of living creatures. Stopping at night beside a shoe repair shop, Merwin notices how the shoes seem to exist on their shelves, and in the opening lines he unravels their hidden history:

> Long after the scheduled deaths of animals
> their skins made into couples
> have arrived here
> empty
> from many turnings
> between the ways of men. (66)

In *Writings to an Unfinished Accompaniment* Merwin's original world seems literally to exist as an animate being. In order to supplant the reader's view of the world as object,

Merwin makes it appear as a subject; he personifies the world, giving it eyes, hands, or tongue, so that it appears as a huge benign creature. For instance, in "The Clear Skies," Merwin discloses that the clouds are eyes, and in so doing he suggests that this view of the world is one that most human beings have lost. "The clouds that touch us out of clear skies," he exclaims: "they are eyes that we lost / long ago on the mountain." In "September" the sights and sounds of the world in autumn lead the poet to perceive its independent existence: "month of eyes," he proclaims, "your paths see for themselves / you have put your hand / in my hand."

Merwin's animate, living world also has a soul or consciousness. It is sentient and feels the presence of human beings, often looking back at them as they look at it. This motif appears in Merwin's "In the Life of Dust," which begins with the statement "Dust thrown into eyes / learns to see." In this poem dust follows two men, watching them "scraping dust from the ground." Dust feels their "footprints running," and, although they are unaware, "it is the dust in front of them / somewhere else waiting / watching." In such tales Merwin fully develops the mythic principle noticed years earlier in his essay on Dylan Thomas—"the vision of man as a metaphor of the world" ("The Religious Poet," 62). That man and world are metaphoric of one another is a way of saying that the world is man's double. Not only does it have human limbs and organs, but it also has a soul, the *Spiritus Mundi*. Through this mythic identification of the world, Merwin emphasizes the unity of mankind and world. In his myth there is no difference or division between them, and neither mankind nor world has any reality without the other. When he looks for himself while shaving in "Shaving without a Mirror," in *Opening the Hand*, Merwin sees no self-image or reflection of himself. Rather he sees the sky and trees, for the world is mankind's alter ego.

Merwin also expresses the relationship between mankind and world through the concept of kinship. In his story the world is mankind's progenitor, an ancient guardian from which he was born. This Romantic motif is heard in such poems as "The Day" in *Writings to an Unfinished Accompaniment*, as Merwin explains how to approach the day and say "Come Father." An animate world that is mankind's kin is a world in which total communication is possible. Indeed, the most striking characteristic of the world in Merwin's story is its need to take on language—to speak. Throughout *The Carrier of Ladders* and *Writings to an Unfinished Accompaniment*, this mythic motif is pervasive. The world's need for language is imaged as "the calling" that is heard around or within things in such poems as "The Lake" or "Beyond You." It is also imaged as "the voice" that compels the poet. Through these expressions of the world's independent life, Merwin reveals the truth of Mircea Eliade's comment about mythic consciousness. "In the last analysis," as Eliade explains it, "the World reveals itself as language. It speaks to man through its own mode of being, through its structures and its rhythms."[1]

The world's actual language is its silence: this is its mode of being. Silence is the aspect of the world's rhythmic motion; it is the song of cosmic harmony that is an "unbreathed music." Through its silent, inspirational gestures the world communicates its celestial dimension, and it seeks to take on actual words by urging the poet to speak for it. Creative activity is for Merwin self-transcending unity with the world; in this experience the world's song is converted into actual language. That neither mankind nor world is complete without this activity is a theme heard often in his poems. In "Words," in *Writings to an Unfinished Accompaniment*, he is explicit about the need for communication between mankind and world:

> When the pain of the world finds words
> they sound like joy
> And often we follow them
> with our feet of earth. (61)

1. *Myth and Reality*, trans. Willard R. Trask (New York: Harper, 1963), 141.

\* \* \*

Merwin may have conceived the idea of a speaking world from the animal poems of *The Carrier of Ladders*. In them he assumes animal identities so that the animals use human language to speak their existence. These poems cap a vein of animal poetry in Merwin's career: in nearly every volume he has written about animals, and some of these poems, such as "Lemuel's Blessing," are among his most intriguing. Taken together these poems form a chapter in his story of an original world: in the mythical first world there is friendship and communication between mankind and animals; but after the Fall there is estrangement from this innocent condition. For primitive people the memory of this condition was restored through efforts to learn animal habits and language. Essentially this is the plot and intention of Merwin's story, for he believes that animals present overwhelming evidence of the world's independent life and of the web in which mankind is one part. Repeated use of animal subjects in his career discloses in his temperament the pull of cosmos over history.

The earliest episodes in Merwin's story of animals retell mythic tales belonging to cultural history. Drawing on ancient and medieval folklore in *A Mask for Janus*, he sets the stage for all of his animal poems by retelling the story of Noah, whom God commanded to save animals from destruction by the deluge. Alluding to this myth throughout his career, Merwin identifies with Noah as he stands amid the ruins caused by historical action and looks for a way to preserve mankind's connection with animals. Referring obliquely to Noah as a type for the poet in "Notes for a Preface," Merwin calls the poet "a summoner" whose task is "to call the next real creatures from the ark" (269).

In Merwin's tale the animals stand in the original world— a meaning suggested by the title of his third book, *Green with Beasts*. Beginning the book with five long animal poems, collectively titled "Chapters for a Bestiary," Merwin draws inspiration from medieval bestiaries in which animals were used to illustrate Christian morals. However, when Merwin writes about such animals as a cock or two goats, he intends to reveal their share in a world that existed before human history. In "Blue Cockerel," for instance, the bird exists in a setting obviously prior to time. Reversing the ancient tale in which the cock marked time, Merwin depicts it as the harbinger of paradise in which time is fixed and endless. "Morning was never here," he claims in the poem's opening line, "but in the fixed green / And high branch of afternoon, this bird balances." As he describes the bird's brilliant plumage and the tree on which it roosts, it is clear that the bird inhabits the celestial earth, where all is fullness and plenitude:

> It seems to be summer. But save for his blue hackles
> And the light haze of his back, there is no sky,
> Only the one tree spreading its green flame
> Like a new habit for heaven . . . (129)

In "White Goat, White Ram," Merwin is more explicit about the world of spiritual presence that animals signify. As the poem begins he watches two goats grazing beside the sea on a hillside. Ruminating on their existence, he concludes that they do not betoken the innocence that human beings have attributed to them. Rather, the goats stand in "the mystery" that is "the world's full age"—the life of the world before humans inhabited it. Existing independently of human attempts to understand them, they call to mind the inadequacy or "dumbness" of such attempts, and they indicate that humans, too, inhabit a mysterious world. "For all our parables, yet the mystery they stand in / Is still as far from what they signify / As from the mystery we stand in." The goats awaken in the poet intuition of the world's celestial dimension, and therefore he asserts that for all we know "a little above us / There are the angels," before whom we appear as dumb creatures. As he concludes the poem, Merwin reaches a kind of mystic transport, for he realizes that he stands on a celestial earth—"for the ground where we find we stand is holy."

In Merwin's story animals reveal mankind to himself, exposing reasons for the Fall from the original world. In "White Goat," for instance, he explores differences between human and animal modes of perception. Without a past or future the animals exist entirely in the present; having no memory, they are incapable of temporal or historical consciousness. Therefore they must understand the world as it is, rather than through learned concepts and signs. Without self-consciousness they perceive no division between themselves and the world. "She sees not summer, not the idea of summer, / But green meanings, shadows, the gold light of now, familiar," Merwin declares of the white goat. He elaborates this mode of perception as one that is simple and entirely of the present in his poem "A Sparrow Sheltering under a Column of the British Museum," in *Green with Beasts*. Observing a sparrow taking shelter from wind behind the museum's massive column, he imagines that the bird knows absolutely nothing of the column's purpose in supporting the building, or of the fact that it is a column. Rather it "knows simply that this stone / Shelters." Because there is no distance from the world in the perception of animals, Merwin was later to make them symbols of creativity.

In contrast to animals, human beings remember their past, and this memory constitutes them as human beings. As Merwin declares in his poem "Learning a Dead Language," "What you come to remember becomes yourself." Humans also project a future on the basis of the past, and therefore their actions become intentional and are often incongruous with the flow of life in the present. For this reason Merwin portrays memory as a faculty isolating mankind from animals and limiting his capacity to see the original world. In a poem in *The Carrier of Ladders*, "Now It Is Clear," he states: "Now it is clear to me that birds vanish because of something I remember." Furthermore, mankind's reasoning intelligence—based on memory—leads him to see the world and its objects in terms of human purposes. By virtue of reason man is able to shape the world into signs and categories so that he will be better able to make his way through it. This domesticating activity is exposed in Merwin's "White Goat," as he observes that human beings made the goats into a sign for innocence in order to categorize their neighbor's behavior.

By domesticating the animals, mankind relegates them to an inferior position in the Creation. Forgetting his primordial relationship with them in which the Creation was equally shared, mankind sees himself as Creation's raison d'être and, therefore, divides himself from the animals. In Merwin's story mankind goes further, waging war against the animals. He pushes them off the planet, then uses his intelligence to justify these erasures of other species. Merwin deals with this brutality in "For a Coming Extinction," a poem in *The Lice*, in which he speaks to the "Gray whale"—an endangered species. Addressing the whale as he would another human being, Merwin instructs him in what to tell the Creator when he reaches "the End." In this place beyond earth and beyond the modern historical moment, Merwin envisions that the whale will meet other extinguished species—"The sea cows the Great Auks the gorillas / The irreplaceable hosts." With bitter irony he tells the whale: "Join your word to theirs / Tell him / That it is we who are important." Merwin's concern for endangered species discloses the ecological emphasis in his myth. Like Gary Snyder, he believes that humanity is threatened by the loss of contact and familiarity with other creatures.

In Merwin's tale the animals ultimately refuse to be tamed or domesticated. Mankind may extinguish them and use them for his purposes, but, because at the beginning he existed alongside animals, he can never ultimately sever his connection with them. Merwin believes that the animals are within: they exist in humanity's preconscious depths and are prior to historical life and the domesticating consciousness in which humans conduct their lives. To suggest the importance of animals, Merwin began at midcareer to mythicize them more heavily, portraying strange creatures who are difficult to name or identify. For instance, in "Lemuel's Blessing" in *The Moving Target*, Merwin addresses a wolf as a "Spirit" as the poem begins: "You that know the way, / Spirit, / I bless your ears which are like cypruses on a mountain." Of the mythical animals in his poems, Merwin has written to the poet Paul Carroll: "These animals are not chosen and refuse to be identified, absolutely, zoologically. They rise . . . from dreams, facing away, and no more want that kind of partial identification than the Other wishes to divulge a name."[2]

"Lemuel's Blessing" is structured on the tension between mythic awareness and the domesticated, historical consciousness. Merwin assumes the mask of a dog—of a creature who has been domesticated by the hand of man. Yet he yearns to escape this condition and prays to the wolf within him, for the wolf is the wild and undomesticated being who is capable of escaping historical life: "without you / I am nothing but a dog lost and hungry," the speaker exclaims. As Merwin develops the poem, the dog-man begs to be delivered from all the domestic postures that attend his sociohistorical identity: "I have sniffed baited fingers," he tells the wolf; they would make him the "faithful custodian of fat sheep." That the wolf-spirit is inward, untamable mythic consciousness emerges in the speaker's prayer near the poem's conclusion: "lead me at times beside the still waters; / There when I crouch to drink let me catch a glimpse of your image / Before it is obscured with my own."

In the final episodes of Merwin's story, the animals become mankind's conscience. He gives them speech, making them talk of the original condition from which mankind is fallen. Stressing their value and necessity, they remind the reader of an originally intimate relationship. In "The Owl," in *The Carrier of Ladders*, the bird declares: "I who / love you / find while I can some light to crawl into." In "Words from a Totem Animal," in the same book, a speaking animal describes his movements in the world of the beginning as it perpetually comes into being. Running in the hills, he ap-

2. Paul Carroll, "Lemuel's Blessing," in *The Poem in Its Skin* (Chicago: Big Table; New York: McGraw-Hill, 1968), 150.

pears as a spiritual creature inhabiting a place where all things are undomesticated and unnamed: "there are no names for the rivers / for the days for the nights," he claims. In his conception of the poem, Merwin took inspiration from the Indian practice of totemism in which certain animals were believed to be supernatural beings combining traits both of spirits and of animals. These spiritual animals, in Indian tales, were world-creators who actually shaped the world's topography. Merwin employs this identity for his speaker, as he recounts primordial, cosmic events: "the soles peeled from my feet and / drifted away / clouds." As the voice of the world-spirit, Merwin's totem animal is ultimately another expression of the Creation's eternal song of life. He is the inspirational voice arising from the poet's sense of unity with the world. As such, the animal is Merwin's "totem"—an idealized creative identity—who utters the poet's creed as he moves toward renewal of vision. "My eyes are waiting for me / in the dusk," he proclaims, "and I am feeling my way toward them."

In "Words from a Totem Animal" Merwin closes the distance between mankind and the animals. By giving the animals speech, he gives them dramatic necessity, bringing alive the intimacy that exists between humans and animals in myths of paradise. Merwin also uses the motif of kinship to assert the importance of their relationship. "Words" alludes to this kinship since the totem animal, in Indian practice, was usually a progenitor and ancestor of the tribe. In "Kin," in *The Carrier of Ladders*, Merwin is explicit. Observing birds coming toward him on a mountain, he states: "it is from them / that I am descended."

The motif of kinship raises questions about Merwin's story of animals. To what extent are division and alienation the result of historical life and therefore capable of being overcome? To what extent are they natural and therefore part of mortality? Merwin suggests an answer in his poem "Cuckoo Myth" in *The Carrier of Ladders*. He relates hearing the voice of the mythical bird, who goads mankind to come to grips with his identity by asking repeatedly "who are you." In the poem the cuckoo's song is the voice of the world-spirit, and Merwin describes how the bird "flew again to the first season / to the undivided." Yet he identifies the cuckoo's song as a voice that will never be clear: "a voice that bears with it its hiding." In this little tale about the origin of the human condition, Merwin indicates that alienation from the original world is an aspect of mankind's mortal status:

> Stay with the cuckoo I heard
> then the cuckoo I heard
> then I was born. (97)

# V. A Mythic Image of Humankind

Merwin's poetry from *The Moving Target* through *Opening the Hand* presents a mythic image of humankind. As mythmaker he answers the root questions of existence by imagining the origin, end, and destiny of the human being. Combining images from Christian, Classical, and pantheistic mythologies, Merwin's account of the human condition is traditional: it portrays the life of the individual as part of an encompassing Creation with a transcendent pattern of meaning. Yet mankind in Merwin's myth is also a unique being set apart from the natural world: he is a restless seeker possessing freedom of choice and bearing responsibility for the creation of his own identity. In this respect, Merwin's account is modern and has affinities with the existentialist image of mankind projected by such thinkers as Søren Kierkegaard, Nicolas Berdyaev, and Martin Heidegger. An existentialist note is also heard in Merwin's myth by virtue of his effort to participate through poetry in what he conceives to be the archetypal life. He is able to imagine his poetic vocation in terms of human destiny.

Mankind's origin is spiritual in Merwin's myth of the human condition. Like the world, each human being comes forth from the source of all being—from the numinous world of possibility and pure freedom. This infinitely creative dimension contains all possible human identity: like a huge ocean of spiritual being, it harbors the souls of the dead and the unborn. These invisible spirits wait to become human in Merwin's "Divinities," in *The Lice*; in fact, this poem restates the mythic theme that gods live mortal lives. As Merwin imagines them, they exist in pure uncircumscribed freedom, because they have yet to enter the objective world:

> Having crowded once onto the threshold of mortality
> And not been chosen

There is no freedom such as theirs
That have no beginning. (59)

Mortal existence in Merwin's tale is objectification—a fall from the original condition of freedom and spirit. At birth each person takes on a body, becoming subject to the limitations and necessities of objective being in time. Yet each remembers the original freedom by virtue of imagination, which for Merwin is the spiritual part of the human being. As though it were a piece of the original freedom, imagination continues to touch the source of existence, to conceive the possibility of immortal being. For this reason each person lives a divided life, having both mortal identity and immortal being. On several occasions in his career Merwin characterizes mankind's divided nature, reformulating the traditional human duality of body and spirit. Stressing mortal identity as contingency in nature and immortal being as creative imagination, Merwin claims in his essay on Dylan Thomas that the human being is "man the creature-creator" ("The Religious Poet," 63); later, in "Notes for a Preface," he refers to "man, the animal and the artist" (272). Like Wallace Stevens, Merwin regards imagination as the supreme faculty—the divinity in each human being.

In Merwin's story mortal existence is a span of time after which one returns to the original condition. At the end of life one encounters death not as a total annihilation of identity but rather as a return to life at the level of immortal being. Merwin imagines his own death in these terms in his well-known poem in *The Lice*, "For the Anniversary of My Death." On the day of death, he claims, his life will be extinguished as if it were one flame in a universe of fire; but part of him will continue, setting out like a "Tireless traveller / Like the beam from a lightless star." Merwin also imagines death as reunification: in death one rejoins the community of spirit composed of ancestors who preceded one on the earth. In "Wharf," in *Writings to an Unfinished Accompaniment*, he describes the experience of death as both an end and a beginning in which one recovers an original unity:

> . . . our gravestones are blowing
> like clouds backward
> through time to find us
> they sail over us through us
> back to lives that waited
> for us
>
> and we never knew. (38)

For Merwin the dead play an important role in the individual's mortal existence. Even in this life communication with them is both necessary and possible. This motif brings to light the traditional emphases in his story, and in fact he is repeatedly inspired by premodern conceptions of death and afterlife. Death, for tribal peoples, is not an event in which the spirit goes far away to another land or heaven. Rather, the spirit remains near the community of the living either waiting to reenter a body being born or lurking in trees or clouds, where it serves as an intercessor for its mortal relatives. Just on the other side of the appearances of things, the dead ask for favors (such as rain) from the great, uncreated god who remains a mystery.[1] In Merwin's story the dead exist within and behind things—in the creative dimension of depth—and he uses the motif of walls or doors to indicate their separation from their mortal brethren. In "February," in *The Carrier of Ladders*, for instance, he is explicit about the presence of the dead behind the world:

> . . . the ends and the beginnings
> are still guarded
> by lines of doors
> hand in hand
> the dead guarding the invisible

1. See Hartley Burr Alexander, *The Mythology of All Races: North American* (New York: Cooper Square, 1964), 190.

each presenting its message
*I know nothing*
*learn of me.* (51)

Communication with the dead in Merwin's story occurs through use of the imagination. Because imagination is freedom and spirit, it can penetrate the wall or door separating the dead from the living. It is the task of imagination to rejoin the dead and to seek their community, and a number of poems in Merwin's later work are based on such an act of communication with dead relatives or friends. "To My Brother Hanson" in *The Moving Target* is one notable example, in which Merwin speaks to his brother who was stillborn; "Voice" in *The Carrier of Ladders* is another, in which he imagines a dead friend, Jane Kirstein, existing on the other side of the wall of appearances. Most often, however, Merwin's imagination seeks community with the anonymous multitude of dead ancestors—with the "long line of ghosts" that he feels passing through him in "Meeting" of *Writings to an Unfinished Accompaniment*. To imagine all the dead is to participate in the total community of human spirit: it is an act both instructive and painful, for one grasps the fact that one's mortal identity is merely one instance of an infinite number of human possibilities. What the dead would have us learn in Merwin's story is that we are not whole or complete by ourselves and must recognize our dependence on the past community of beings. In *Writings to an Unfinished Accompaniment*, Merwin's "A Wood" expresses his tale of mortal existence as separation from a community of spirit. "I have stood among ghosts of those who will never be / because of me," he claims.

"A Wood" also reveals the estrangement and angst that for Merwin inform mortal existence. Even though imagination conceives unity of being, the individual person cannot feel complete merely because he exists. Since it is impossible for matter to become spirit, each is bound to feel a painful sense of division and fragmentation in mortal life. In Merwin's story mortal existence and imaginative being are associated with paired motifs expressing life's division and its contradictory impulses. Existence is grief: it is feeling incomplete. To exist is to realize that one is bound to the earth and is consequently subject to error and limitation. In contrast, imaginative being is hope: it is a feeling of wholeness and perfection. To hope is to feel the reality of immortal being conceived by imagination. Merwin also associates mortal and immortal being with the mythic motifs of falling and flying. To exist is to fall: after the original fall at birth, each person continues to fall away from the source of being and from memory of it. But to imagine is to fly—to escape mortality's falling and to return to the source in an act of self-renewal. In imagination one attains a godlike perfection of being transcending the actualities of objective identity.

Merwin also uses the mythic symbol of wings to refer to life at the level of imagination. In his image of the human being each one has a wing with which to hope and to fly. Yet when Merwin uses the wing as an image, he usually undercuts the possibility of pure flight. In "Foreword" in *Writings to an Unfinished Accompaniment*, he tells a tale of human origins, making mankind "the orphan" with only one wing: "everything here has two wings / except us," he relates, suggesting the limitations of mortality. "Is That What You Are," a poem in *The Lice*, brings together images of hope, grief, and flight to express life's division and the impossibility of ultimately surmounting it. In this poem Merwin characterizes mankind as a being who has two wings: one of hope, the other of grief. The poem is addressed to a ghost who appears before the poet, seeming to encourage him to use his wings to fly. Yet when he tries he finds flight impossible:

New ghost is that what you are
Standing on the stairs of water
. . . . . . . . . . . . . . . . . . . .
Hope and grief are still our wings
Why we cannot fly

What failure still keeps you
Among us the unfinished. (4)

The presence of the new ghost in Merwin's poem suggests a crucial theme. However impossible it may be in this
life to transcend the limitations of mortal existence, it is the
destiny of each human being to continue making the effort.
For Merwin human identity emerges in the confrontation
between spiritual being and mortal existence. As the spiritual side, imagination challenges the mortal being, urging
him to go beyond what he factually is or what he has
achieved as a historical creature. Imagination conceives
perfection of identity because it touches on the source of
infinite human potential, and it demands that each mortal
being become perfect by making actual all his possibilities.
In the course of life, identity is realized, as one historicizes
as much as possible of one's spiritual being. That human
identity is dynamic constitutes the moral dimension of
Merwin's tale.

Merwin structures a number of interesting poems on the
confrontation of spiritual being and mortal existence. In
them the confrontation takes the form of a dialogue as he
addresses one side of himself or the other, echoing such
Yeatsian poems as "A Dialogue of Self and Soul." In "Finally," a poem in *The Moving Target*, he addresses the mortal side of himself, expressing dissatisfaction with the accu-
mulated weight of habit and of error to which it is subject.
Wishing to transcend this mortal identity and to achieve a
pure and more perfect mode of being, he declares as the
poem begins: "My dread, my ignorance, my / Self, it is
time. Your imminence / Prowls the palms of my hands like
sweat." Stating that he will place between himself and his
mortal identity "the old knife" that symbolizes their con-
tinuous struggle, the speaker implores the mortal self to be
reconciled to the possibilities of the best self. "Come," he
asserts, "Let us share / Understanding like a family name."
Merwin's "Animula" in *The Carrier of Ladders* is similarly
structured, yet this poem clearly expresses the division of

human nature as one between body and soul. Using the traditional term *soul*, Merwin yearns for immortal being— for the experience of self-unity that is beyond being in time. "Look soul / soul / barefoot presence," he declares in the opening lines. "I will take you," he continues, to "the river we / know"—to the spiritual river of being—where "the nights are not separate."

Because spiritual being is inexhaustible possibility, the challenge of realizing identity is never completed in this life. No sooner is an action taken to secure identity than the spirit creates another possibility and demands its realization. In Merwin's story this perpetual challenge makes life a voyage or journey. The moment of birth is the moment of departure in which one begins to move through life in time in search of the spirit. In "On Each Journey," in *Writings to an Unfinished Accompaniment*, Merwin imagines the spirit as silence: "on each journey there is / a silence that goes with it / to its end." In other poems he conceives the body as a boat in which to sail forth in pursuit of spiritual being. This mythic motif is heard in "For Saying that It Won't Matter," a poem in *Writings to an Unfinished Accompaniment*, which, like "Animula," is structured on the dialogue between existence and immortal being. Speaking as the spiritual part of himself, Merwin addresses his own bones. He imagines the hour of death when they will separate and he will leave his body "on the empty shore." "Bones of today I am going to leave you," he warns: "you are voyaging now through the half light of my life / let us talk of this while the wind is kind / and the foam rustling on your bows."

In Merwin's tale it is the spirit that is the true voyager. Conceiving new possibilities of identity, the spirit seems to be always escaping and going before the mortal being, out into the future. As the demand of future identity, the spirit seems literally to call: it is the calling being who is always ahead—beyond the time and place in which one finds himself. In Merwin's "Late Night in Autumn," in *The Carrier of Ladders*, the call comes from the poet's soul in order to remind him that his identity is incomplete and his journey unfinished. Thinking of the passing of time and of those who are satisfied with objective identity, Merwin claims:

> the year will soon be home and its own hear it
> but in some house of my soul
> a calling is coming in again off the cold mountains
> and here one glove is hanging from each window
> oh long way to go. (112)

\* \* \*

These lines also reveal the demands of Merwin's poetic vocation. The calling comes both from the soul and from "the cold mountains" because it is the eternal song given to the poet to create. Over and over, imagination hears this inexhaustible freedom and possibility from which all things come to be. For Merwin it is the ultimate good that can never be fully conceived or named by the human mind. Poetic vocation is to make this limitless reality into poetry as often as is possible for one mortal being. Through imagination, the imagemaking faculty, one names it repeatedly by describing its presence in the visible world. In this act one becomes immortal, for art, in Merwin's myth, immortalizes the poet. Art is the record of his imaginative life—of his unity with the creative dimension. In it he ceases to exist as a mortal, achieving an identity beyond time and place and taking a position in human culture—in the mind of the world.

In Merwin's mythic self-conception, a poet must live the life of an immortal being. Like the divinities, he must obtain for himself conditions insuring pure creative freedom. In order that imagination be free to move toward all that is unrealized, it must be protected from the distractions and the inhibitions that are normally part of mortal existence. Finally, creative freedom requires that a poet purge imagination of all culturally determined images: these are the names given to the creative dimension by one's nation or religion and learned as a part of one's mortal condition. To secure this freedom, Merwin has avoided the mode of life associated with American poets after World War II. Shunning academic positions, he has not taught in a university, and he has spoken out against the proliferation of creative writing programs as a way of learning how to write poetry.[2] He has also refused to write much criticism and to partake in poetic movements. In Merwin's conviction all such activities are objectifying: they delimit creative imagination and threaten to obscure what he terms "the 'freedom' that accompanies poetry at a distance" ("On Open Form," 272).

Merwin has also followed through on his conception of the immortal poet as an exile. Like Robert Graves or Samuel Beckett, he has lived apart from his homeland, residing since 1978 in Haiku, Hawaii, and returning only occasionally to the American mainland. In the last analysis Merwin's effort to preserve creative freedom discloses in his personality a hereditary Protestantism. Despite conscious rejection of his father's creed and his antipathy to its narrowing orthodoxy, he was apparently influenced by the root principle of Protestant thought—by its original premise of reform. The impulse of Protestantism is radical change and reform because it does not believe that any man-made creed can circumscribe the unconditional reality that is god. Eventually it abolishes all myths and creeds in the vision of a god who is "wholly other," to use the words of the Protestant theologian Karl Barth.

Merwin mythicizes personal identity in his poems to express his conception of the poet as an immortal being. He creates two mythic identities that are variations on the theme of the immortal poet. The most prominent identity is that of the pilgrim-traveler: the poet is one who passes through life in search of the higher truth. For Merwin travel means creative freedom. To travel is to transcend mortal existence and to escape the domestic life that through habit and custom blunts imagination's capacity to see the world

2. David Ossman, *The Sullen Art: Interviews by David Ossman with Modern American Poets* (New York: Corinth, 1963), 68.

anew. In his earliest volume, *A Mask for Janus*, Merwin asserted this mythic theme by prefacing it with an epigraph from the American writer John Wheelwright: "Habit is evil, all habit, even speech / And promises prefigure their own breech." In later career Merwin is explicit: it is the poet's fate to travel. "I am the son of farewells," he declares in "Fourth Psalm," in *The Carrier of Ladders*; and in "Nomad Songs," in *Writings to an Unfinished Accompaniment*, "my cradle / was a shoe." Through the title of his second volume of prose, *Houses and Travellers*, Merwin calls attention to his sense of himself as world-traveler: he is the poet who journeys around the world, stopping to make houses—a symbol for constructions of imagination that become part of human culture.

The mythic identity of the traveler also expresses Merwin's need to resist self-complacency. The most dangerous inertia is inward, arising from success as a poet—from what Merwin terms in "Lemuel's Blessing" the "ruth of approval." After publication every poem or book contributes to mortal identity; bringing recognition as a poet, it leads one to believe that one has achieved vocation. For Merwin, however, the call to be a poet is never-ending because there are innumerable possibilities of expression. The immortal poet will regard each book as a kind of death: as an encrustation on pure freedom that must be left behind so that the next one can be written. This concept of an inward pilgrimage to realize one's possibilities is heard in such poems as "Travelling" in *Writings to an Unfinished Accompaniment* and "Envoy from D'Aubigne" in *The Carrier of Ladders*. Written on the occasion of publishing a book, the latter poem portrays the mortal poet ceaselessly dissolving identity so that the immortal poet might create in freedom: "I think of all I wrote in my time / dew / and I am standing in dry air."

Merwin also characterizes immortal being in poetry through the mythic identity of the mountain climber. Like flying, climbing is a motif that expresses the human capacity for rising out of the confusion and desire of mortal experience. Using mountains and plateaus as actual images, Merwin casts himself as one who rises to accept the challenge of spiritual being: like a god on Mount Olympus, he embraces the cold and rarified air of the heights. This episode in his story derives from the Asian myth mentioned in Chapter I in which a magic mountain joined earth to heaven. At the summit of this mountain creation began and from there it continued spreading outward; this was the locus of the original world where gods, men, women, and animals existed in harmony. Merwin also uses the North American Indian myth that the mountain peak was the abode of gods and spirits; the Indians buried their dead high up the slopes in a village of the dead. Merwin alludes to this belief in "Ascent," a poem in *The Carrier of Ladders*. "I have climbed a long way," he claims as the poem begins. It is clear that in this climb he has transcended mortal identity, for he directs the reader's attention to his shoes far below, which "wait there looking up." His goal is to reach the high slope—"the bare meadows"—in which there is community of spirit. There he will know himself seen "by the lost / silent / barefoot choir."

In Merwin's latest poetry there is a retreat from the posture of the immortal poet. *The Compass Flower*, *Finding the Islands*, and *Opening the Hand* initiate a new phase in his career in which poetic identity is based on mortal existence. To be sure, Merwin occasionally claims mythic identity. "One Night," in *Opening the Hand*, begins with his declaration: "I ride a great horse climbing / out of a rose cloud / onto a black cinder mountain." Furthermore, almost all Merwin's latest work continues to be inspired by the myth of a transcendent creation threatened by the destructive progress of modern history. Yet when Merwin faces either nature or the sociohistorical world, he expresses his subject less and less as myth: he allows his imagination less creative freedom with which to transfigure and reorder what appears. Instead actual events are realistically described, and frequently these events are occasions in the personal life of the poet. Depicting a sociable poet who often shares the poem's experience, Merwin's latest poetry is "occasional": it is produced from the poet's senses and from his conscious mind.

Much of Merwin's later poetry moves further toward explicit self-revelation and autobiography. In *The Compass Flower* he begins to demonstrate interest in himself, the well-known poet W. S. Merwin: he falls back on the fact that there is an audience who would like to read about his personal life. Such poems as "Ferry Port" and "Masts" concern travel, yet the act of traveling has no inward necessity. Instead Merwin merely relates his itinerary. "Ferry Port," for instance, begins with this revelation from the mortal poet: "We will be leaving now in less than a week / meanwhile we are / staying in a house in the port." The tendency of the poet simply to describe continues in poems like "Visitation" in *Opening the Hand*.

*Finding the Islands* includes a section of thirteen poems that concern Merwin's domestic life with an intimate loved one. The presence of this woman in his life is first felt in poems of *The Compass Flower*, but in them Merwin mythicizes the relationship. He eliminates specific details of their life together and identifies the woman with the Earth-goddess, who offers unity of being. In *Finding the Islands* Merwin's treatment of love is confessional: he casts himself as a man who feels love and desire rather than as a cold immortal being. "When we get home / from wherever it is / we take off our clothes," he asserts in "Living Together"; in "At Home," he states, "I find you cooking / in your torn / underpants worn low."

In *Opening the Hand* Merwin appears more as a mortal being than ever before in his career. In this volume there is an initial section of nineteen poems that are based on personal memories of his family. The poems ought to be read in conjunction with his third prose volume, *Unframed Originals* (1982), a series of six autobiographical memoirs of his boyhood life in Pennsylvania and New Jersey. Merwin's design in the poems, as in the prose, is to be more "open"; hence the title *Opening the Hand*. He has suspected for years that he is too retiring and reticent, especially since, through implication, he has been so accused by his commentators. In the latest work he looks for this character trait in his family, and in what he regards as an oppressive paternal influence. Having exposed his father's mother as the typical American puritan, Merwin portrays his father as a poser and social climber. To Merwin his father's ways were harsh and tyrannical, and he feels that his father failed to appreciate his special talent of imagination—a fact evident in his poem "Houses" in *Opening the Hand*. Further, Merwin blames his father for hiding from him the details of the family's history, especially those that were less than socially proper. His father suppressed his knowledge of life's gaiety and color, to the point of preventing contact with vivacious and fun-loving relatives. This indictment emerges in "Birdie," a poem about Merwin's aunt, whom his father never fully accepted, and who therefore epitomizes "the way we grew up to hide things from each other."

Yet Merwin seems uncertain about becoming an "open," mortal poet. The form and style of his three latest books suggest this uncertainty. While such volumes as *The Lice* were stylistically homogeneous with all poems contributing to a unity of effect, in the latest there is a range of experimentation with both line and stanza; there is also a division of each book into sections of poems organized around different themes. More explicit uncertainty can be heard in such poems as "The Truth of Departure" and "Emigre" in *Opening the Hand*. In the latter poem Merwin addresses a "you," who is clearly in one sense himself. He wonders about the value of his self-exile and the impact it has had on his use of language. Revealing that America has become to him "a category," he broods on the question, "what is your real / language." Implicitly he poses a more encompassing question: does pure freedom from one's culture undermine verbal communication which is based upon community? In this long self-revealing poem that is its own subject, Merwin also questions the value of his most recent poetic subject—personal memory. Here the value of self-revelation in poetry is implicitly being debated:

> what of the relics of your childhood
> should you bear in mind pieces
> of dyed cotton and gnawed wood
> lint of voices untranslatable stories
> . . . . . . . . . . . . . . . . . . . . . .
> or should you forget them
> as you float between ageless languages
> and call from one to the other who are you. (76)

Merwin's uncertainty about poetic identity, and about the place of personal experience in the poem, reflects an uncertainty characteristic of American poetry in the post-modern era. Originally the postmodern movement sought to recapture experience of the world. As a continuing reassertion of Romanticism, it reacted against the over-civilized human consciousness—against "academic poetry" having little to do with actual experience. Writers such as Bly, James Wright, and Merwin himself were successful in realizing postmodern theory, which held that the artist would break down artificial barriers between the human subject and the world. From the beginning, however, heavy emphasis fell on the human subject rather than the world. In one main direction of the postmodern movement, poets concentrated on personal identity and activity in a familiar human realm. Represented by such poets as Robert Creeley, this direction became dominant in the 1970s: with the "personalization of poetry" the poet rendered his actual, everyday experience without allusion or mythification. Personal experience as the subject of the poem was its own justification, as poets said by implication to their readers: "I am my own myth."[3]

This direction in American verse is not surprising. In democratic nations poetry tends toward autobiography. It is produced from the familiar contents of consciousness

3. A. Poulin, Jr., "Contemporary American Poetry: The Radical Tradition," In *Contemporary American Poetry* (Boston: Houghton, 1971), 389, 393.

and concentrates on human customs and on the surface of life. As de Toqueville suggested in the 1840s, the democratic poet will be a mortal being. He will be a familiar, casual person, not a man searching mountains for his soul. Merwin's latest work is in step with this literary direction. Undoubtedly he is aware that if he is to immortalize himself through poetry his work must be read and appreciated. Yet in terms of quality his latest poems are not distinguishable from the bulk of contemporary American poetry. Merwin's poetic talent—his potential as a major poet—is based on "conditions of mythology." As these conditions involve transformation of the world, they are rarely actual or familiar.

## WORKS BY W. S. MERWIN

### Poetry

*The Carrier of Ladders*. New York: Atheneum, 1970.
*The Compass Flower*. New York: Atheneum, 1977.
*Finding the Islands*. San Francisco: North Point, 1982.
*The First Four Books of Poems: A Mask for Janus, The Dancing Bears, Green with Beasts, The Drunk in the Furnace*. New York: Atheneum, 1975.
*The Lice*. New York: Atheneum, 1967.
*The Moving Target*. New York: Atheneum, 1963.
*Opening the Hand*. New York: Atheneum, 1983.
*Writings to an Unfinished Accompaniment*. New York: Atheneum, 1973.

### Prose

*Houses and Travellers*. New York: Atheneum, 1977.
*The Miner's Pale Children: A Book of Prose*. New York: Atheneum, 1970.
*Unframed Originals*. New York: Atheneum, 1982.
"Favor Island." In *New World Writing 12*. New York: Mentor-New American, 1957.

### Articles

"Among the Rats." Review of *La Guerre d'Algerie*, by Jules Roy Julliard. *The Nation*, 5 November 1960, 351–52.
"Act of Conscience: The Story of *Everyman*." *The Nation*, 29 December 1962, 463–80.
"Notes for a Preface." In *The Distinctive Voice: Twentieth Century American Poetry*, compiled by William J. Martz, pp. 268–72. Glenview: Scott, 1966.
"On Open Form." In *Naked Poetry: Recent American Poetry in Open Forms*. Edited by Stephen Berg and Robert Mezey, pp. 270–72. Indianapolis: Bobbs-Merrill, 1969.
"On the Bestial Floor." *The Nation*, 22 March 1965, 313–14.

"The Relevance of Some Russians." Review of *Roots of Revolution: A History of the Populist and Socialist Movements in Nineteenth Century Russia*, by Franco Venturi. *The Nation*, 23 September 1961, 182–84.

"The Religious Poet." In *A Casebook on Dylan Thomas*, edited by John Malcolm Brinnin, pp. 59–67. New York: Crowell, 1960. Reprinted from *Adam International Review* (1953).

"To Name the Wrong." *The Nation*, 24 February 1962, 176, 178.


Translations

*Asian Figures*. New York: Atheneum, 1973.

*Euripides: Iphigenia at Aulis*. Translated with George E. Dimock, Jr. New York: Oxford University Press, 1978.

*Four French Plays*. New York: Atheneum, 1984.

*From the Spanish Morning*. New York: Atheneum, 1984.

*The Life of Lazarillo de Tormes, His Fortunes and Adversities*. With an Introduction by Leonardo C. de Morelos. Garden City, N.Y.: Anchor-Doubleday, 1962.

*Osip Mandelstam: Selected Poems*. Translated with Clarence Brown. London: Oxford University Press, 1973.

*Poem of the Cid*. With an Introduction by W. S. Merwin. 1959; rpt. New York: Mentor-New American, 1962.

*Products of the Perfected Civilization: Selected Writings of Chamfort*. With a Foreword by Louis Kronenberger and an Introduction by W. S. Merwin. Toronto: Macmillan, 1969.

*Sanskrit Love Poetry*. Translated with J. Moussaieff Masson. New York: Columbia University Press, 1977.

*The Satires of Persius*. With an Introduction by William Anderson. Bloomington: Indiana University Press, 1961.

*Selected Translations, 1948–1968*. New York: Atheneum, 1968.

*Selected Translations, 1968–1978*. New York: Atheneum, 1979.

*Some Spanish Ballads*. London: Abelard Schuman, 1961.

*The Song of Roland*. With an Introduction by W. S. Merwin. 1963; rpt. New York: Vintage-Random House, 1970.

*Transparence of the World: Poems by Jean Follain*. New York: Atheneum, 1969.

*Twenty Love Poems and a Song of Despair*. By Pablo Neruda. Cape Editions 38. New York: Grossman, 1969.

*Vertical Poetry: Poems by Roberto Juarroz*. Santa Cruz: Kayak, 1977.

*Voices: Antonio Porchia*. Chicago: Big Table, 1969.